D0040059

FIGURES OF
SPEECH

FIGURES OF SPEECH

FIRST AMENDMENT HEROES AND VILLAINS

WILLIAM BENNETT TURNER

Foreword by Anthony Lewis

PoliPointPress

Figures of Speech: First Amendment Heroes and Villains

Copyright © 2011 by William Bennett Turner

All rights reserved, including the right to reproduction in whole, in part, or in any form.

15   14   13   12   11   1   2   3   4   5

Production management: BookMatters
Book design: BookMatters
Cover design: Charles Kreloff
Cover photo: Corbis

Library of Congress Cataloging-in-Publication Data
   Turner, William Bennett.
   Figures of speech : first amendment heroes and
   villains / by William Bennett Turner.
      p.   cm.
      Includes bibliographical references and index.
      ISBN 978-1-936227-03-7 (alk. paper)
      1. Freedom of speech—United States.
   2. United States. Constitution. 1st Amendment.
   I. Title.
   JC591.T85   2011
   323.44'3092273—dc22   2010041916

Published by:
PoliPointPress, LLC
80 Liberty Ship Way, Suite 22
Sausalito, CA 94965
(415) 339-4100
www.p3books.com

Distributed by Ingram Publisher Services
Printed in the USA

*For Molly and Andy, who always
wanted to know more than I knew,
and for Micki, who saved my life*

CONTENTS

FOREWORD

The First Amendment has become the hottest battlefront of American constitutional law. Libel, campaign spending, publication of government secrets, hateful speech: these and a dozen other subjects have tested the amendment's command that "Congress shall make no law . . . abridging the freedom of speech, or of the press." The very words "First Amendment" have become a rallying cry for the press and other interests arguing that their freedom outweighs other public concerns. As a result of First Amendment litigation, activities commonly regulated or prohibited in other democracies—denunciation of religious groups, leaks of military records, political advertising—are now protected by the Constitution.

The literature of the First Amendment has grown apace. Books on interpretation of the fourteen words in its speech and press clauses are numerous; I have added to the pile myself. But this book is different. It does not have the smell of the lamp, of theorizing at a distance. It is a report from the front lines.

Here are men and women whose often eccentric lives led to great courtroom tests of freedom: Yetta Stromberg, who had a red flag when she was a counselor at a summer camp for young Communists in 1929 and was sentenced to prison for displaying that symbol of radicalism. And Dannie Martin, a longtime criminal who wrote articles for the *San Francisco Chronicle* about the federal prison he was in until the authorities stopped him.

Bill Turner is a First Amendment lawyer. (I use the nickname because I have known him for many years.) He shows what goes on in a case before a court hands down a decision. He gives intimate and fascinating details of lawsuits that he personally tried and argued, and of others going back into history.

Yetta Stromberg's case, for example. What anyone is likely to know about it is the decision of the United States Supreme Court in 1931. Chief Justice Charles Evans Hughes, writing for the Court, tells us that Ms. Stromberg was convicted of violating a California law that made it a crime to display a red flag "as a sign, symbol or emblem of opposition to organized government." Hughes said that "a fundamental principle of our constitutional system" is that there should be opportunity for "free political discussion to the end that government may be responsive to the will of the people and that changes may be obtained by lawful means." The California law violated that principle.

Turner fills in the picture of Yetta Stromberg—and of what we might think was the naïve radicalism of her summer camp. Yetta, 19 years old, and the other counselors were all volunteers. At seven every morning red flags were raised, and Yetta led the campers in reciting: "I pledge allegiance to the workers' red flag, and to the cause for which it stands. . . ."

Then Turner gives us a glimpse of the political context that produced this case. Yetta's camp was raided by a California district attorney, accompanied by carloads of vigilantes—American Legion members looking for subversives. They arrested Yetta and six others, including Bella Mintz, the camp cook. A jury convicted Yetta and five others, and she was sentenced to prison for one to ten years.

In short, Yetta was a victim of the Red Scare that gripped much of America in the 1920s. California and dozens of other states passed laws condemning the red flag and criminalizing what they called "syndicalism"—Communism or socialism by another name. A succession of challenges to these laws reached the Supreme Court, but through that decade they were rejected by a conservative majority of the Court. The contrary case—the case that unpopular speech must be allowed in a constitutional democracy—was made by two dissenting justices, Oliver Wendell Holmes Jr. and Louis D. Brandeis. The supreme example of their logic and their rhetoric was Brandeis's opinion in the 1927 case of Anita Whitney, who had been convicted in California of belonging to an organization that advocated "criminal syndicalism." Brandeis wrote:

"Those who won our independence . . . believed liberty to be the secret of happiness and courage to be the secret of liberty. They believed that freedom to think what you will and to speak as you think are means indispensable to the discovery and spread of political truth. . . . Believing in the power of reason as applied through public discussion, they eschewed silence coerced by law. . . ."

The dissents of Brandeis and Holmes finally became the voice of the majority on the Supreme Court in the case of

Yetta Stromberg. In his opinion reversing her conviction, Chief Justice Hughes did not rise to the eloquence of Holmes and Brandeis. But his conclusion that the California red flag law violated the constitutional principle of free political discussion was a decisive victory for the First Amendment. It was, as Turner points out, the first time ever that a claim of free speech had won a constitutional test in the Supreme Court. And it was the beginning of a steady expansion of that freedom by the Court over the following decades.

We must not be too romantic, however, about judges as defenders of our freedom. The Red Scare of the 1920s was by no means the only time large numbers of Americans gave way to fear. Fear of Communism gripped the country during the Cold War, when Senator Joseph McCarthy and other demagogues thrived on Communist-hunting. And the Supreme Court was slow to stand against the threat to freedom.

The lowest ebb of First Amendment protection during the second Red Scare came in 1951, when the Supreme Court upheld the conviction of American Communist Party leaders for conspiring to teach the necessity of overthrowing the government. The party was a feeble remnant by then, and it posed no imaginable threat. Justice Hugo L. Black, dissenting, said: "Public opinion being what it is now, few will protest the conviction of these Communist petitioners. There is hope, however, that in calmer times, when present pressures, passions and fears subside, this or some later Court will restore the First Amendment liberties to the high preferred placed where they belong in a free society."

Later Supreme Courts did exactly that, breathing new life into the First Amendment. But Turner reminds us that the law of freedom is not made only by those nine justices in Washington. It is made by nasty characters like Larry Flynt of *Hustler* magazine. It is made by reporters like Earl Caldwell of the *New York Times*, who resisted the government's demand that he appear before a grand jury to be questioned about his coverage of the Black Panthers. And it is made by lawyers like Bill Turner, guiding clients through the toils of official resistance to the uplands of freedom.

Anthony Lewis

INTRODUCTION

Dramatis personae

This is a strange cast of characters: Communists, Jehovah's Witnesses, Ku Klux Klansmen, prison wardens, James Madison, dogged reporters, federal judges, the world's leading pornographer, a computer whiz, and others. Some of them are First Amendment heroes. Some are First Amendment villains. Some of them are famous; most are obscure. All played a role in a controversy contributing to our modern understanding of freedom of speech.

First Amendment controversies are often started by colorful characters. Many of them are not nice or polite; nor do they have noble motives. They say, or want to say, mean or disturbing things, speech that people don't want to hear. Some want to speak truth to power, but the powerful want them silenced. Very few people are pure First Amendment heroes, that is, people who want to advance the cause of free speech for everyone. We all say we believe in free speech—in the abstract, or when it's our own speech or a point of view we agree with. We're not so sure when it's speech that expresses ideas that we loathe.

Most would-be First Amendment speakers—people who claim constitutional protection—have their own agendas, and those agendas are often at odds both with majoritarian sentiment and with societal values other than freedom of speech. Nothing is wrong with that: a free country is supposed to work that way.

First Amendment heroism and villainy, as in the rest of life, are about courage and cowardice. The heroes are those who say what they believe, insist on saying it even when people (and governments) don't want to hear it, and have the courage to face the consequences. Villains are those who want to suppress speech they disagree with or are fearful of, or who give in too easily to competing values and go along with the idea that this is speech people shouldn't have to hear.

This book is about people who intentionally or accidentally became First Amendment heroes or villains. These are my idiosyncratic selections. Undoubtedly others are worthy of the honor or the badge of infamy. I chose some of the heroes and villains from my personal experience with them, and to that extent this book is a memoir. The book also sums up most of what I have learned from working on and teaching First Amendment cases.

■　　■　　■

For the last quarter century, I have taught the First Amendment at the University of California at Berkeley, the home of the Free Speech Movement in the 1960s. These days, however, fewer Berkeley undergraduates seem to care about free speech. They seem too ready to embrace the competing values offered to restrict speech, and many seem too respectful of authority in general. Being respectful of authority is of course at war with First Amendment values. We don't need a First Amendment to protect our right to read White House press releases. We do need one to uncover and disclose abuses of power, to protect speech that most people don't want to hear, and to debate what kind of country we want to be.

Indifference to how and why we protect civil liberties is distressingly widespread. A recent study found that only half of high school students say newspapers should be allowed to publish freely without government approval of stories. One-third say the First Amendment goes "too far" in guaranteeing free speech. Former Supreme Court Justice Sandra Day O'Connor recently gave a speech lamenting young people's ignorance of how our fundamental values are protected. She said, "Knowledge about our government is not handed down through the gene pool. Every generation has to learn it, and we have some work to do." O'Connor complained that "Two-thirds of Americans know at least one of the judges on the Fox TV show 'American Idol,' but less than 1 in 10 can name the Chief Justice of the United States Supreme Court." I have tested this in my class, and the situation is a little worse than O'Connor thought: almost all 110 Berkeley students in the class knew the American Idol judges, and only a couple could name Chief Justice John Roberts.

■   ■   ■

Speech in the United States has always been relatively free, but it has never been an absolute freedom. You don't in fact have the right to say whatever you want, whenever and wherever. Libel and perjury are pure speech but illegal. Government has always imposed restrictions and always asserts that competing values require suppression of particular speech. For example, the information, if made public, will endanger national security; the hate speech will incite violence; the online sexual material will harm our children; tabloid journalism will destroy privacy, and so on. In other words, every time government tries to restrict speech, it does so in the name of competing values. Free speech is not the only important value in our society. It frequently collides with other values, important interests that we all care about. That's what makes First Amendment controversies so hard, and so interesting.

The accepted wisdom is that free speech deserves Constitutional protection because it serves three purposes: it advances knowledge and the ascertainment of truth, facilitates self-government in a democracy, and promotes individual autonomy, self-expression, and self-fulfillment. Truth-seeking occurs when everyone can speak freely in a marketplace of ideas, a marketplace in which the government must remain neutral; government can't be allowed to suppress what it considers bad ideas—we don't get to the truth by muzzling dissenters. Free speech is essential to self-government, a system in which we the people are sovereign, for we must be able to criticize government and the officials whom we elect to serve us. Bill Clinton once said, wistfully, "It's almost a citizen responsibility to criticize the President. . . . Why be an American if you can't criticize the President?" Free speech makes it possible non-violently to change the government, the laws, and those who govern (just as Watergate reporting brought down President Nixon). Individual self-fulfillment is a basic human value and is good in itself, apart from the utility of free speech in helping to find the truth and in facilitating democracy.

A couple of reminders about the First Amendment: *First*, only government can violate it. Our Constitution is a series of constraints on the power of government, and government alone. It does not bind corporations, labor unions, churches, or private entities of any kind. No matter how vague and oppressive Facebook's or Yahoo's "terms of use" are, no matter how much they restrict free speech, they do not violate the First Amendment. That's because these corporations are not the government. No matter how much corporations insist on conformity to the corporate "culture" and forbid employees from publicly saying what they think, this does not violate the First Amendment.

People who should know better sometimes fail to understand First Amendment basics: especially that only government is barred from abridging free speech. Sarah Palin got it upside down during the 2008 presidential campaign. Feeling that the mainstream media were unfairly criticizing her for negative statements about Barack Obama (like his relationship with Rev. Jeremiah Wright), she complained, "I don't know what the future of our country would be in terms of First Amendment rights and our ability to ask questions without fear of attacks from the mainstream media." But the media can't violate her First Amendment rights, and media "attacks" on political candidates are the exercise of First Amendment rights, not their abridgment. The First Amendment doesn't protect candidates from press criticism—it encourages it.

Second, what the First Amendment means is what the

Supreme Court says it means. The simple text of the amendment ("Congress shall make no law . . . abridging the freedom of speech, or of the press") does not provide the answers to any modern free-speech controversies. The answers come from the Court when it rules on the issues that are brought to it by the parties in concrete cases. The question for the Court in a First Amendment case is whether the particular speech comes within "the freedom of speech" protected by the amendment. This decision essentially involves evaluating whether some competing societal value justifies restricting the speech in question.

Case in point: *Citizens United*

The Supreme Court's 2010 decision on corporate speech and campaign finance reform is a vivid example of the collision of competing values and the Court's role as decider. *Citizens United v. Federal Election Commission* was the most important First Amendment decision of the 21st century so far.

The 5–4 decision threw out, on its face, part of the McCain-Feingold package of reforms, specifically the federal campaign finance law that prohibited corporations and unions from using their funds on communications—mainly television advertising—that support or oppose a candidate for office. The case pitted the value of unrestricted political speech against the need to keep corporate money from contaminating elections. The decision came down squarely on the free-speech side, or the corporate side, depending on how you look at it.

The liberal establishment was outraged. There were calls for a constitutional amendment, and the *New York Times* printed a nearly hysterical editorial. Bloggers warned that the ruling unleashed corporations to buy whatever candidates and legislation they like and lamented that electoral power would be shifted from the promising new grassroots social networking innovators to reactionary corporate interests. An altered formal portrait of the Court circulated on the Internet, showing the robes of the five majority justices festooned with corporate logos as if they were NASCAR drivers. People for the American Way said the Court "staged a hostile takeover of American democracy on behalf of corporations."

I too have long been disgusted with the influence of money on politics. Elected officials and office-seekers seem to devote more time and energy to fund-raising than to governing, and clearly their positions on legislation are influenced by the interests that back them financially (whether through direct contributions, PACs, or lobbyists). I'm unhappy with any decision that increases the dominant role of money in the political system.

On the other hand, I teach and believe in the First Amendment as one of the most distinctive and important values of our society. I view suspiciously any restriction on political speech. Any restriction should be rigorously tested, not given the benefit of the doubt.

Justice Anthony Kennedy's opinion for the Court brushed aside all procedural obstacles to the broadest possible decision. The case involved a conservative nonprofit corporation, Citizens United, that produced a 90-minute documentary, "Hillary: The Movie," and wanted to make it available for video-on-demand. The film was an attack on then-Senator Clinton, intended to sabotage her in the 2008 presidential primaries. As characterized by the Court, the film was "a feature-length negative advertisement that urge[d] viewers to vote against Senator Clinton for President." Citizens United sued the Federal Election Commission (FEC), contending that the federal law did not *apply* either to it, to video-on-demand, or to the documentary. It formally *stipulated* in the district court that it did not challenge the law *on its face*.

The Supreme Court, however, refused to interpret the law narrowly, rejected any "as applied" approach, overruled two of the Court's recent precedents, and declared the federal law invalid *on its face*. It was a decision of breathtaking scope. Campaign finance reformers were livid.

Many critics of the decision focused on the conservative majority's hypocrisy in abandoning all judicial restraint to reach a decision broadly condemning the law. Justice John Paul Stevens, then almost 90 years old, observed in his 90-page dissenting opinion that the majority had improperly "manufactured" a facial attack on campaign finance laws: "Essentially, five justices were unhappy with the limited nature of the case before us, so they changed the case to give themselves an opportunity to change the law." Reminiscent of his dissent from the similar judicial power grab in *Bush v. Gore* (awarding the presidency to George W. Bush), Stevens said of the majority, "[The] path it has taken to reach its outcome will, I fear, do damage to this institution." Advocating judicial restraint while practicing raw, unadorned, result-oriented judicial activism will earn the public's distrust.

Apart from the majority's activism, what seemed to bother people about the merits of the *Citizens United* decision was its supposed reliance on two fictions: that "money is speech" and that "corporations are persons" with free-speech rights. But these turn out to be more complicated subjects. Obviously money is not speech, but the Court did not in fact say that it is. Quoting its earlier decision in *Buckley v. Valeo*, it said that a "restriction on the amount of money a person or group can spend on political communication during a campaign . . . necessarily reduces the quantity of expression by restricting the number of issues discussed, the depth of their exploration, and the size of the audience reached." This seems self-evident. To "speak" in an election campaign requires you to spend money: to print pamphlets and mail them to voters; to design and print posters and distribute them to locations where they will be seen; to rent space on billboards; to advertise on radio and television, and so on. Banning expenditures on electioneering communications, or restricting the amount that can be spent, unquestionably silences political speech. This does not necessarily mean that spending money must be treated as the exact equivalent of standing on a soapbox for all purposes. But condemning the Court for having said or decided that "money is speech" is misleading and more slogan than analysis.

But should *corporations* have free-speech rights? Corporations are not people, don't think, don't have beliefs, and can't vote. Why should they be able to claim a First Amendment right to "speak" in elections? Justice Kennedy pointed out how broadly the prohibitions swept. The law applied not just to Fortune 500 giants with billions in assets but to all 5.8 million for-profit corporations, most of which are relatively small businesses, many with a sole shareholder. It applied to labor unions large and small. Equally sobering, it applied to all *non*profit corporations, including advocacy organizations, making it a crime for any of them to run an ad supporting or opposing a candidate. As Kennedy put it,

> The following acts would all be felonies: The Sierra Club runs an ad, within the crucial phase of 60 days before the general election, that exhorts the public to disapprove of a Congressman who favors logging in national forests; the National Rifle Association publishes a book urging the public to vote for the challenger because the incumbent U.S. Senator supports a handgun ban; and the American Civil Liberties Union (ACLU) creates a Web site telling the public to vote for a Presidential candidate in light of that candidate's defense of free speech. These prohibitions are classic examples of censorship.

The prevailing theme of Justice Kennedy's opinion was that "the First Amendment does not allow political speech restrictions based on a speaker's corporate identity." The emphasis is on the speech, not on the speaker. *If* it is true that corporations have the same speech rights as natural persons, the Court's decision that they can't be restricted from spending on core political speech was clearly correct.

The human need for self-expression, one of the values served by free speech, of course has no application to corporations: they can't, by "speaking," satisfy this human need and, conversely, denying them the benefit of free speech does not impair this interest. If their right to speak is to be recognized, it must be because it serves different First Amendment purposes, such as encouraging free and critical debate about government and leading citizens to the truth by exposing them to diverse points of view in a marketplace of ideas. The majority in *Citi-*

zens United certainly thought allowing corporate speech served these purposes.

Having emphasized that free political *speech*, not the corporate identity of the speaker, is what the First Amendment is about, Kennedy concluded that the federal prohibitions were not narrowly tailored to serve the campaign reform interests that the government claimed. Indeed, at one point Kennedy virtually said reformers might as well give up: "Political speech is so ingrained in our culture that speakers find ways to circumvent campaign finance laws." Kennedy said that while an "appearance of influence or access" may stem from corporate political spending, this "will not cause the electorate to lose faith in our democracy." (Perhaps he had his fingers hopefully crossed on this one.) Justice Stevens saw it very differently: "The Court's blinkered and aphoristic approach to the First Amendment" will promote corporate domination of the election process. He added that "Americans may be forgiven if they do not feel the Court has advanced the cause of self-government today. . . . While American democracy is imperfect, few outside the majority of this Court would have thought its flaws included a dearth of money in politics."

Putting aside the unseemly route the Court took to get to its sweeping decision, the uncritical endorsement of corporate speech, and the likely exacerbation of the problem of money in politics—does the decision have redeeming First Amendment values? On the merits the decision is a very strong statement of fundamental First Amendment principles. Justice Kennedy, who in my view has been the strongest member of the current Court on the First Amendment, used his opinion to reaffirm and expand on several bedrock tenets of the freedom of speech.

Many of the tenets emerged from First Amendment battles waged by the heroes whose stories are told in this book and benefit all of us. It is good to be reminded of them:

- Kennedy proclaimed, "Speech is an essential mechanism of democracy, for it is the means to hold officials accountable to the people." Further, "[The First Amendment] has its fullest and most urgent application to speech uttered during a campaign for public office." To attack or support a candidate is of course core political speech.

- Kennedy almost said political speech can't be restricted at all "as a categorical matter" but backed off to say that at least any restriction is subject to "strict scrutiny," which requires the government to prove that the restriction "furthers a compelling interest and is narrowly tailored to achieve that interest." This tough standard is virtually the kiss of death for whatever legislation is under scrutiny, as it was in *Citizens United*.

- "More speech, not less, is the governing rule." This proposition harks back to Justice Louis Brandeis's classic 1927 opinion in *Whitney v. California*. The idea is that if government is concerned about subversive, erroneous speech that may mislead the people, "the remedy to be applied is more speech, not enforced silence."

- Justice Kennedy's emphasis throughout his opinion was on the importance of protecting political *speech* regardless of who the *speaker* may be. The reasoning was that in a democracy we the people are entitled to hear all points of view and that government should not be allowed to disfavor speech based on who is speaking. This idea is "premised on mistrust of governmental power."

- Justice Kennedy declared, "Prolix laws chill speech for the same reason that vague laws chill speech: people of common intelligence must necessarily guess at the law's meaning and differ as to its application." This is new. The Court had long recognized that *vague* speech regulations, especially those that carry criminal sanctions, improperly chill speech. But "prolix" laws? The campaign finance law thrown out by the Court was a mess; it was exceedingly complex, and would-be speakers had to confront not only the less-than-crystalline language of the statute but 568 pages of FEC regulations, 1,278 pages of explanations, and 1,771 FEC advisory opinions. Treating prolixity as a subspecies of vagueness is good for the First Amendment and for all of us.

- In the same vein, the Court said that as a practical matter, a speaker who does not want to risk criminal or civil liability for campaign speech is effectively forced to seek an advisory opinion from the FEC. Justice Kennedy said having to "ask a government agency for prior permission to speak" is "the equivalent of prior restraint"; it gives the FEC "power analogous to licensing laws implemented in 16th- and 17th-century England, laws and governmental practices of the sort that the First Amendment was drawn to prohibit." This was somewhat overstated, but it was nice to see the Court reaffirm the free-speech principle first recognized in the classic 1931 case of *Near v. Minnesota* that "prior restraints"— government censorship of speech before it is uttered—are unconstitutional.

- Finally, for those who would expand First Amendment freedoms regardless of competing values, it actually was good that the Court bulldozed its way through all the procedural obstacles to declare the law invalid on its face and was willing to overrule precedents that restricted speech. The Court previously had said that invalidating a law passed by Congress on its face is "strong medicine" to be sparingly used, even in free-speech cases. *Citizens United* will be a strong precedent for future challenges to various kinds of speech regulation.

The *Citizens United* result is distressing because this impressive catalog of fundamental First Amendment principles was put to the service of corporate interests rather than to assist the lonely individuals who invoke the amendment to *challenge* the power structure. The dispossessed, eccentrics, minorities, and dissidents are the ones who need the First Amendment's help, not society's established institutions.

A cynic might plausibly consider *Citizens United* a *faux* First Amendment decision, a pro-business effort dressed up in free-speech clothes. Justice Kennedy himself allowed some pro-business leaning to show through, remarking that the restriction on corporate spending "muffled the voices that best represent the most significant segments of the economy." Referring to candidates' electoral speech, he said, "On certain topics corporations may possess valuable expertise, leaving them the best equipped to point out errors." Except for Kennedy, the other members of the conservative majority have not previously exhibited great attachment to free-speech values. (Eight days before its *Citizens United* decision, the very same five-justice majority intervened on an emergency basis in another case with First Amendment implications. The Court summarily prohibited streaming television coverage of the Proposition 8 same-sex marriage trial in San Francisco to other federal courthouses. The disingenuous ground it gave for its ruling was that the district court had allowed only 5 days for public comment on a change in its local rules instead of the 30 days that was usually given. This departure from the local rules was trivial and inconsequential. In fact, the court had received 138,574 public comments, all but 32 favoring transmission. The Supreme Court recognized that district courts can adopt and amend local rules governing how they do business. The majority's rationale for reversing the district court, however, was this: "If courts are to require that others follow regular procedures, courts must do so as well." How quickly the five majority justices forgot about "regular procedures" in *Citizens United* and threw off the bonds of judicial restraint to rule for business interests.)

The four conservatives who joined Kennedy to decide *Citizens United* all came to Washington as part of the Reagan revolution and have been fully committed to its anti-government regulation ideology: getting government off the backs of business. They all subscribed to the Federalist Society agenda of free enterprise unlimited by nettlesome government restrictions. Intrusive and detailed campaign finance laws and regulations must have seemed repugnant to their beliefs. The cynic might suspect that their real allegiance was to the Reaganesque agenda of freeing business from government regulation rather than to the loftier values of free speech. At any rate, they are very different from the kinds of First Amendment heroes we meet in this book.

■   ■   ■

First Amendment freedoms are fragile, since they are always threatened by competing values—from campaign finance reform to national security to public decency—and those values change over time. The freedoms that we now have—as exhibited by the principles recited and reinforced in the *Citizens United* case—were not created yesterday out of whole cloth. Nor did they spring into being upon the ratification of the First Amendment in 1791. Our current freedoms are the products of the kinds of First Amendment controversies, mostly in the last few decades, described below. Recognizing that every First Amendment dispute involves the collision of competing values—else there would be no dispute—let's turn to the First Amendment heroes and villains to see how their stories inform the contemporary meaning of the First Amendment.

· 1 ·

YETTA STROMBERG

Yetta Stromberg was 19 years old when she was a counselor at a summer camp for young Communists. It was 1929. The camp was in the mountains near San Bernardino, California. The campers came from working-class Communist families from Los Angeles. The 40 or so boys and girls ranged in age from 6 to 16. The parents paid only $6 a week per camper, as all the adults at the camp, including Stromberg, were volunteers.

At 7:00 every morning, Stromberg led a flag-raising ceremony for the campers. As the children stood by their beds, one of them would raise a red flag while the others recited in unison this pledge:

> I pledge allegiance to the workers' red flag,
> And to the cause for which it stands,
> One aim throughout our lives,
> Freedom for the working class.

On August 3, 1929, the camp was raided by several carloads of American Legion members from nearby Redlands, led by George H. Johnson, the district attorney of San Bernardino County. The raid was prompted by the Better America Federation of Los Angeles and the Intelligence Bureau of the Los Angeles Police Department, who were keeping a close eye on radical activities. The Federation, backed by business interests, believed the republic was being undermined by a subversive conspiracy directed by Bolsheviks in the Soviet Union.

When the raiders arrived, some children were playing baseball, some were off hiking, and some were studying economics under the leadership of Yetta Stromberg, who had been a student at UCLA. On the hillside, the raiders found a flagpole and a homemade triangular red flag on which someone had painted a black hammer and sickle. They also discovered a cardboard box labeled "Please do not touch," which contained some sheet music and some Communist literature. It belonged to Stromberg but was for her own reading and use, and the children did not know about it. The raiders confiscated the flag and the literature, and they arrested six women and one man. Besides Stromberg, those arrested were Emma Schneiderman, who played the piano; Sarah Cutler, Emma's mother who was visiting the camp for the day; Jennie Wolfson, the camp manager; Esther Karpeliff, who washed and cleaned up; Bella Mintz, the cook; and Isadore Berkowitz, the handyman.

The arrestees were taken to jail in San Bernardino. They were charged with violating a California law enacted in 1919, during the Bolshevik scare, that made it a felony to display a red flag in a public or meeting place "as a sign, symbol or emblem of opposition to organized government or as an invitation or stimulus to anarchistic action or as an aid to propaganda that is of a seditious character."

The California law was not an aberrant outlier. Thirty-two states passed similar laws in the Red-Scare era following World

War I. The proponents of this kind of legislation were not concerned about any infringement of First Amendment freedoms. They were consumed by fear of anarchists, Communists, and radical labor leaders. The values that inspired these laws were patriotism, loyalty, and national unity. Opposition to government and these "American" values was to be punished by the criminal law.

At the trial of the *Stromberg* case in October, 1929, the centerpiece of the prosecution's case was the box of Stromberg's Communist literature. Though no testimony was presented indicating that anyone but she knew what was in the box, Judge Charles L. Allison allowed the prosecutor to read all of the literature to the jury. The Legionnaire raiders testified about finding the flag.

The jury returned a verdict of guilty against all the defendants except Sarah Cutler, the visiting mother. Yetta Stromberg was convicted of both conspiring to display the red flag and actually displaying it. Before sentencing, a steel heiress named Kate Crane Gartz of Altadena, who was a champion of unpopular causes, wrote Judge Allison a letter asking, "Could you not tell as you listened to Yetta that she was a young woman of high principles and ideals and not a criminal fit only for crucifixion?" She also asked the judge to "go easy with these young enthusiasts." Allison cited Gartz for contempt of court and fined her $75. (For this act alone, the judge qualifies as a First Amendment villain.)

Stromberg was sentenced to prison for a term of one to ten years. She and the others appealed. The American Civil Liberties Union (ACLU), which the Better America Federation considered a front for Soviet interests, handled the appeal. The

California Court of Appeal set aside the conspiracy convictions but affirmed the judgment against Stromberg alone for displaying the flag. The ACLU took her case to the United States Supreme Court.

On May 18, 1931, the Court handed down its decision. Led by Chief Justice Charles Evans Hughes, the Court focused on the California law's prohibition of flying a red flag as a symbol of opposition to organized government. Hughes emphasized that a "fundamental principle of our constitutional system" is the opportunity for "free political discussion to the end that government may be responsive to the will of the people and that changes may be obtained by lawful means." In other words, Americans *do* have the right to oppose our government, and the ability to advocate change is integral to what makes us a free people. Chief Justice Hughes concluded that the law was so vague and indefinite that it permitted punishment of those who use the opportunity to oppose government. The statute was therefore "invalid upon its face," and Yetta Stromberg's conviction was set aside.

■   ■   ■

Stromberg might have been surprised to learn that her case, *Stromberg v. California,* was the first time in American history that the Court had struck down a law on First Amendment grounds. Why did this take almost a century and a half? One reason is that until the Fourteenth Amendment was added to the Constitution after the Civil War, the First Amendment did not apply to the states. The First Amendment says that *"Congress* shall make no law . . . abridging the freedom of speech, or of the press," and this was deemed to apply only to the fed-

eral government, not the states. Any state and local laws that
restricted speech therefore did not violate the First Amendment. Although the states had their own constitutions with
protections for speech and press, the federal Constitution left
them free to restrict speech if they wished. Southern states,
for example, criminally prosecuted those who advocated the
abolition of slavery, and no one suggested that this violated the
First Amendment.

The adoption of the Fourteenth Amendment in 1868 had no
immediate effect. It expressly applied to the states and prohibited them from depriving any person of "life, liberty or property" without due process of law. But not until 1925, in another
of the Red-Scare cases, did the Court first interpret the term
"liberty" in the Fourteenth Amendment to include the freedom of speech and press as protected by the First Amendment.
In other words, First Amendment freedoms were incorporated
into the Fourteenth Amendment and became applicable to the
states in the same way they are applicable to the federal government. The decision in the 1925 case, *Gitlow v. New York,*
was bittersweet for Benjamin Gitlow, its hero or victim. He
was a leader in the Socialist Party who was prosecuted under
a New York state "criminal anarchy" law for publishing "The
Left Wing Manifesto." The manifesto called for overthrowing
organized government and establishing a "revolutionary dic-
tatorship of the proletariat." Gitlow won the vitally important
constitutional point that applied the First Amendment to the
states. Unfortunately for him, however, the Court's majority
decided that advocacy of radical action was not within the
freedom of speech protected by the First Amendment, and
Gitlow went to prison. Although the constitutional precedent

was small consolation for Gitlow, it opened the door for Yetta Stromberg to win her case in the next decade.

Another reason why other speech-restricting laws had not been thrown out by the Court before *Stromberg* was that between the infamous Sedition Act of 1798 and the First World War, Congress had not passed any. The Sedition Act, enacted in an excess of patriotism on the Fourth of July, made it a crime to defame the president or Congress. The act was an attempt by the Federalist administration under President John Adams to muzzle the Republican press and prevent the party led by Thomas Jefferson and James Madison from taking power. Fourteen men, mostly editors of Jeffersonian newspapers, were prosecuted and jailed under the act. But its constitutionality was never decided by the Court. The act expired by its own terms on March 3, 1801, the day before the next president, Jefferson, was inaugurated. Jefferson promptly pardoned all the convicted editors, and none of the cases had reached the Court. But as the Supreme Court said more than a century and a half later in *New York Times v. Sullivan*, the Sedition Act was condemned "in the court of history." Jefferson explained that he pardoned the convicted men because he considered the act "to be a nullity, as absolute and palpable as if Congress had ordered us to fall down and worship a golden image." In addition to the Jefferson pardons, Congress passed legislation compensating the editors' families. A consensus developed that the act was antithetical to First Amendment values. The experience with the act taught the lesson that criticizing government was an American right, not a reason to punish a citizen. Congress apparently learned its lesson and did not again attempt anything like the Sedition Act until the First World War. Wartime pressures, combined with hysteria about Bolshevik revolution, led to a rash of federal and state loyalty laws, like those used to prosecute Yetta Stromberg and Benjamin Gitlow. These laws ushered in a wave of litigation about the extent to which government can suppress subversive speech. Thus began the process of defining the modern First Amendment.

■ ■ ■

Yetta Stromberg's case was unusual in another way and made an important contribution to the scope of First Amendment freedoms. Flying a flag was not, on the face of it, "speech." It was not words. It was conduct. Yet it was expressive. It was clearly meant to convey ideas. In Stromberg's case, flying the flag was meant to express solidarity with the working class, support for the Communist system, and opposition to the capitalist system. Indeed, the California statute itself singled out displaying a red flag as a symbol of opposition to organized government; this was the basis for treating this conduct as a felony. The Supreme Court in the *Stromberg* decision, with hardly any discussion, concluded that Stromberg's expressive conduct should be treated as "speech" protected by the First Amendment.

Stromberg's case thus expanded First Amendment freedoms. The seed planted by *Stromberg* sprouted and grew into the "symbolic speech" doctrine used decades later in cases involving burning draft cards, the American flag, and crosses, and students flying a banner proclaiming "Bong Hits 4 Jesus."

In the 1960s, when David Paul O'Brien burned his draft card on the steps of the South Boston courthouse to protest the Vietnam War, the Supreme Court recognized that the "communicative element" in O'Brien's conduct implicated First Amendment speech values. But the Court ruled against him because it found valid the argument that the nonspeech elements of destroying his draft registration document frustrated government purposes (such as identifying and keeping track of draft-eligible young men). When high school students in Des Moines wore black armbands to show their opposition to the war and were suspended, the Court ruled that the discipline violated the First Amendment. It treated the armbands as symbols of political significance and said school officials could not single out the wearers for punishment: "[In] our system, state-operated schools may not be enclaves of totalitarianism."

When Gregory Lee Johnson burned an American flag at the Republican National Convention in Dallas to protest Reagan administration policies, the Court treated his act as "expressive conduct," noting that it had "long recognized that [First Amendment] protection does not end at the spoken word," citing *Stromberg*. The Court said Johnson "was prosecuted for his expression of dissatisfaction with the policies of this country, expression situated at the core of our First Amendment values." The Court rejected the state's argument that burning the flag undermined support for a competing value, national unity, proclaiming, "If there is a bedrock principle underlying the First Amendment, it is that the government may not prohibit the expression of an idea simply because society finds the idea itself offensive or disagreeable." Yetta Stromberg would have been proud (though, ironically, she could not have expected such a result under a Communist system).

When some St. Paul teenagers sneaked into the yard of an African American family and burned a cross (that's not First

Amendment heroism), they were charged with violating an ordinance making it a crime to display a "symbol," including a burning cross or a Nazi swastika, knowing that this would arouse alarm or anger on the basis of race or religion. Once again the Court, in a surprising opinion by Justice Antonin Scalia, reminded everyone that government cannot outlaw speech "or even expressive conduct, because of disapproval of the ideas expressed." Justice Scalia added that "nonverbal expressive activity can be banned because of the action it entails, but not because of the ideas it expresses." The Court concluded that while burning a cross on someone's lawn may be illegal under other laws (such as those that prohibit trespassing), government cannot outlaw an act because it disapproves of the racial or religious ideas it is meant to express.

When Joseph Frederick, a Juneau, Alaska, high school student, unfurled a banner across the street from the school as the 2002 Olympic torch parade passed by—a banner that said "Bong Hits 4 Jesus"—and then was suspended by the principal, no one questioned that waving the banner was an example of free "speech." But Chief Justice Roberts found for the Court that the banner conveyed the wrong message; it was neither core political or religious speech, nor just harmless nonsense. Roberts decided that the principal could reasonably conclude that the banner promoted illegal marijuana use, and public school officials had the power to suppress this message.

So disputes about the extent of protection for symbolic speech or expressive conduct continue. Stirring spirited and provocative discussion about public issues is one of the purposes of the First Amendment. Yetta Stromberg's little red flag admirably served that purpose.

• 2 •

JEHOVAH'S WITNESSES

My constitutional law professor, the great Paul Freund, remarked in class that it seemed most of constitutional law was made by the milk industry and the Jehovah's Witnesses. Indeed, the milk industry was frequently involved in disputes over such Commerce Clause issues as state and local laws establishing minimum prices, requiring local pasteurization, protecting against out-of-state competition, and so on. These cases were possibly of economic significance but were not thrilling for law students to read.

The Jehovah's Witnesses cases, on the other hand, raised issues that go to the heart of what it means to be an American. You might expect the cases to involve the religious clauses of the First Amendment. But in fact the most important decisions have been based on the Free Speech Clause. The decisions do not simply protect the Witnesses' right to practice their religion but protect the freedom of speech for all of us.

The Witnesses have been prolific Supreme Court litigants, accounting for an astonishing 72 decisions by the Court. They are unlikely users of the legal system, believing as they do that all the answers are in the Bible, not in law books. They proclaim that they "believe in the Bible as the Word of God. They consider its 66 books to be inspired and historically accurate." Based on their interpretation of Scripture, they avoid all involvement in politics, discourage voting, and refuse to serve on juries or in the military.

Their role as First Amendment heroes has been somewhat forced on them. One of the obligations placed on Witnesses is to preach and proselytize. They take literally the mandate of the Scriptures: "Go ye into all the world, and preach the gospel to every creature" (Mark 16:15). As their literature says, "You may have seen them on the street, offering their magazines to passersby. Or you may have spoken briefly with them at your door." Indeed, greeting strangers on street corners to hand out their Watchtower leaflets and going door to door to preach and distribute their literature are activities that have not endeared the Witnesses to many towns and their residents, and officials have tried to enact laws to rid them of this "nuisance."

It all started in 1938 when Witness Amy Lovell was arrested in Griffin, Georgia, for distributing literature without first obtaining written permission from the city manager as required by the town ordinance. Lovell had not applied for a permit, as she regarded herself as sent by Jehovah to do his work. She was convicted and sentenced to 50 days in jail.

The Supreme Court reversed Lovell's conviction, finding that the ordinance was "invalid on its face." The law prohibited distributing any kind of literature—newspapers, magazines, leaflets—at any time or place and in any manner without the permission of a government official. It thus struck "at the very foundation of the freedom of the press by subjecting it to license and censorship." Treating the Witnesses as "the press" might seem odd, as I am sure the Witnesses saw themselves as delivering eternal verities, not the news of the day. Using the pamphlets of Thomas Paine and others to illustrate the point, the Court said: "The liberty of the press is not confined to newspapers and periodicals. It necessarily embraces pamphlets and leaflets [which have been] historic weapons in the defense of liberty. . . . The press . . . comprehends every sort of publication which affords a vehicle of information and opinion." (Presumably that would include 21st-century bloggers.)

The broad principle established by *Lovell v. City of Griffin*— that the exercise of First Amendment freedoms cannot be made subject to licensing and government approval—has often been invoked by magazine and film distributors, civil rights and antiwar demonstrators, and others. ("Parading without a permit" was a favorite excuse for local authorities to try to shut down demonstrations.) The principle also serves as a caution to those who see the press as arrogant and irresponsible and wish to impose accountability by licensing journalists the way states license lawyers, doctors, plumbers, and barbers. We have always assumed that government could not license reporters, but the Jehovah's Witnesses case made it law.

Not long after *Lovell*, three Jehovah's Witnesses were arrested in New Haven, Connecticut, and charged with violating a state law that prohibited religious soliciting without a certificate from a government official; they also were charged with breach of the peace. They were going door to door in a heavily Catholic neighborhood, passing out their literature and playing a phonograph record of one of their books. The record was of a book called *Enemies*, which was an attack on "all organized religious systems as instruments of Satan and injurious to man," but singled out Catholicism in terms likely to offend Catholics. In *Cantwell v. Connecticut*, the Court reversed the convictions. It invalidated the statute as an impermissible "prior restraint" on speech because it prohibited solicitation unless the state official determined that "the cause is a religious one" and issued a permit. And it found no breach of the peace: there was no "clear and present" danger from the Witnesses' conduct—no "threatening of bodily harm, no truculent bearing, no intentional discourtesy, no personal abuse."

▪   ▪   ▪

Jehovah's Witnesses established not only the right to speak, preach, and proselytize. They also established the First Amendment right *not* to speak. Unlike Yetta Stromberg and her red flag–saluting campers, the Witnesses believe that a flag is a "graven image" that they are religiously forbidden to "bow down" to. Accordingly, they refuse to salute the American flag, recite the Pledge of Allegiance to it, or sing "the Star Spangled Banner."

In the patriotic fervor of World War II, public school districts throughout the country began requiring flag salutes as part of students' daily routine. When the West Virginia Board of Education instituted a mandatory pledge of allegiance and Jehovah's Witnesses refused to participate, their children were expelled and threatened with being sent to reformatories, and parents were threatened with prosecution for causing delinquency. The Supreme Court stepped in and taught a few civics lessons. In an eloquent opinion, Justice Robert Jackson pointed out, "We are dealing with a compulsion of students to declare a belief." The issue was whether in our democracy the majority may compel citizens to state patriotic beliefs that they may not hold. Justice Jackson noted: "The very purpose of a Bill of Rights was to withdraw certain subjects from the vicissitudes of political controversy, to place them beyond the reach of majorities and officials. . . . [F]ree speech . . . and other fundamental rights may not be submitted to vote; they depend on the outcome of no elections."

Rejecting the state's argument that the flag salute promoted national unity (foreshadowing the state's argument in the Texas flag-burning case in Chapter 1), Justice Jackson said national unity is unquestionably a value that officials may foster "by persuasion and example," but they may not do so by coercion. Moreover, to illustrate how compelling unity of belief is ultimately futile, Jackson provided examples:

> the Roman drive to stamp out Christianity as a disturber of its pagan unity, the Inquisition, as a means to religious and dynastic unity, the Siberian exiles as a means to Russian unity, down to the fast failing efforts of our present totalitarian enemies. Those who begin coercive elimination of dissent soon find themselves exterminating dissenters. Compulsory unification of opinion achieves only the unanimity of the graveyard. . . . It seems trite but necessary to say that the First Amendment to our Constitution was designed to avoid these ends by avoiding these beginnings. . . . We set up government by consent of the governed, and the Bill of Rights denies those in power any legal opportunity to coerce that consent.

As a result of the 1943 decision, Jehovah's Witnesses' children could not be compelled to salute the flag. More generally, the decision confirms that citizens cannot be compelled to say what they do not believe: "If there is any fixed star in our constitutional constellation, it is that no official, high or petty, can prescribe what shall be orthodox in politics, nationalism, religion, or other matters of opinion or force citizens to confess by word or act their faith therein."

Justice Felix Frankfurter wrote a spirited dissent in the West Virginia case. The lone Jewish member of the Court, Frankfurter started on a very personal note: "One who belongs to the most vilified and persecuted minority in history is not likely to be insensible to the freedoms guaranteed by our Constitution." Frankfurter's thesis was a classic statement of judicial conservatism. He argued that a judge's "own opinion about the wisdom or evil of a law should be excluded altogether when one is doing one's duty on the bench." The judge's duty was not to evaluate whether a law was sound policy, as Frankfurter states: "As a member of this Court, I am not justified in writing my private notions of policy into the Constitution, no matter how deeply I may cherish them." Judges can't act as though they are a "super-legislature." This principle of "judicial self-restraint" limits the power of courts to declare laws unconstitutional even though passed by democratic majorities (a principle given short shrift in the 2010 *Citizens United* case). Constitutionality is not synonymous with wisdom, and courts have to accept that there will be unwise laws restricting speech. Justice Frankfurter asserted: "Much which should offend a free-spirited society *is* constitutional" and counseled that instead of looking to the courts to invalidate bad laws, one should rely on the "convictions and habits and actions of a community" to guard against "temptations to fetter the human spirit." Frankfurter's views were principled, but wrong. His approach of giving almost complete deference to legislatures would put the rights of dissidents and racial and religious minorities at the mercy of majoritarian sentiment.

■　■　■

A variation on the right-not-to-speak problem came up in a more recent Jehovah's Witnesses case and has become a 21st-century issue. New Hampshire's automobile license plates are embossed with the state motto: "Live Free or Die." Witness George Wooley objected to being "coerced by the State into advertising a slogan which [he found] morally, ethically, religiously, and politically abhorrent." He put duct tape over the motto on his plates, and was convicted of a misdemeanor for doing so. In the Supreme Court, referring back to the Witnesses' World War II–flag-salute case, Chief Justice Warren Burger said: "We are [again] faced with a state measure which forces an individual as part of his daily life—indeed constantly while his automobile is in public view—to be an instrument for fostering public adherence to an ideological point of view he finds unacceptable." The Court concluded that the license plate requirement violated the Witnesses' right to "refrain from speaking: [T]he freedom of thought protected by the First Amendment [includes] both the right to speak freely and the right to refrain from speaking at all." Forcing a citizen to be a "mobile billboard" for the state's ideological message "invades the sphere of intellect and spirit which it is the purpose of the First Amendment [to] reserve from all official control," quoting the flag-salute case.

License plate speech is also a current issue. With the advent of customized specialty plates offered by many states, politically controversial mottos can, at the owner's option, be embossed on the plates. Twenty or so states now offer Choose Life plates. Illinois, while offering specialty plates for college alumni, hunters, sports fans, and a salute to President Obama, refused to offer a Choose Life plate. Naturally, both offering what appear to be anti-abortion plates and refusing to offer them has resulted in litigation. In Illinois, anti-abortion activists claimed discrimination against their speech; the state argued it wished to remain neutral on the abortion issue. On October 5, 2009, the Supreme Court declined to hear the Illinois case. Unlike the Jehovah's Witnesses case, the new license plate cases do not involve coerced speech; they ask whether government must allow motorists to subject the rest of the public to state-sponsored political statements with which many people may morally or politically disagree. The Court will not be able to resolve these cases without confronting the precedents established in the Jehovah's Witnesses cases.

■   ■   ■

Alas, not every trip to the Supreme Court by the Jehovah's Witnesses resulted in advancing our First Amendment freedoms. When Walter Chaplinsky was proselytizing on the streets of Rochester, New Hampshire, he attracted a restless crowd by denouncing all organized religion as a "racket." A city marshal warned him to "go slow" since listeners were getting upset. A police officer led Chaplinsky toward the police station without arresting him. On the way, they encountered the same city marshal. In an argument about whether anyone should be arrested (including unruly listeners), Chaplinsky called the marshal a "goddamned racketeer" and "a damned Fascist," adding for good measure, "the whole government of Rochester are Fascists or agents of Fascists." Chaplinsky was prosecuted under a state law prohibiting anyone from addressing "any offensive, derisive, or annoying word to any other person" in a public place or calling him "by any offensive or derisive name." His appeal was decided in 1942.

The Supreme Court upheld the conviction. The Court reasoned:

> There are certain well defined and narrowly limited classes of speech, the prevention and punishment of which have never been thought to raise any Constitutional problem. These include the lewd and obscene, the profane, the libelous, and the insulting or "fighting" words—those which by their very utterance inflict injury or tend to incite an immediate breach of the peace. . . . [S]uch utterances are no essential part of any exposition of ideas, and are of such slight social value as a step to truth that any benefit that may be derived from them is clearly outweighed by the social interest in order and morality.

Thus was born the fighting-words exception to freedom of speech. The Court invented an entire category of speech which, like obscenity and libel, has no First Amendment protection. It did so without any evidence that Chaplinsky's outburst caused any harm at all or even offended the city marshal (who might be presumed to have a thicker skin than most). The Court took it as obvious that the names that Chaplinsky called the law enforcement officer were "epithets likely to provoke the average person to retaliation" and a breach of the peace. The Court concluded that fighting words bear no relationship to the search for truth and therefore can be excluded from the First Amendment marketplace of ideas—they are not ideas.

The fighting-words doctrine carries great peril for free speech, allowing law enforcement officers to arrest speakers of angry words, even when the words do not result in violence, on the ground that courts deem them to be of "slight social value." It's always dangerous for judges to be the arbiters of what speech is valuable and what isn't.

Labeling Walter Chaplinsky a First Amendment villain on the ground that the fighting-words limitation on speech is attributable to him would not be fair. It was the Court's mistake. Fortunately, the Court in subsequent cases has partially rectified the mistake by narrowly limiting *Chaplinsky*. Since 1942 no conviction has been sustained by using the fighting-words doctrine, and later cases have interpreted *Chaplinsky* as requiring a direct tendency to cause violence by the person to whom epithets are addressed face to face, not by an offended audience. These cases have also emphasized that courts cannot outlaw words without considering the *context* within which they are used.

Moreover, the categorical approach to free-speech protection—assuming that speech falls into protected or unprotected categories—has not found favor in the Court's modern First Amendment jurisprudence. Instead of simplistically looking to see if certain speech falls within a particular category, the Court is more likely to look closely at the factual context of each case and to balance the individual's interest in the particular speech against the state's interest in suppressing it, to weigh the competing values. Indeed, in the decades since *Chaplinsky* the Court has narrowed all of the previously identified categories of unprotected speech. In addition to closely confining the fighting-words exception, the Court has limited the category of obscenity to hard-core material that meets the Court's three-part definition (see Chapter 8). The Court also has narrowed the category of libel, holding in *New York Times v. Sullivan* and its progeny that false statements defaming public officials and figures do not lose First Amendment protection unless they basically amount to deliberate lies. And the Court refused to expand the unprotected category of child pornography, holding unconstitutional Congress's attempt to ban "virtual" child pornography—images that do not use real children in their production (see Chapter 8).

On April 20, 2010, the Court rejected the government's claim that depictions of animal cruelty should constitute a new category of unprotected speech. Seizing on *Chaplinsky*'s idea that some speech is of "slight social value" and therefore merits no protection at all, the government urged that "crush videos" and other pictures of cruelty to animals should be treated the same as child pornography—wholly without First Amendment protection. The government asked the Court to create an unprotected category by "balancing . . . the value of the speech against its societal costs." Chief Justice Roberts, in his opinion for the Court in the 8–1 decision, found that this "free-floating test for First Amendment coverage" was "startling and dangerous." The free-speech guarantee extends beyond categories of speech that "survive an ad hoc balancing of relative social costs and benefits. The First Amendment itself reflects a judgment by the American people that the benefits of its restrictions on the government outweigh the costs. Our Constitution forecloses any attempt to revise that judgment simply on the basis that some speech is not worth it." No "freewheeling authority" exists to "declare new categories of speech outside the scope of the First Amendment." The decision sounds the death knell for expanding the categorical approach to speech regulation.

The Court in the animal videos case, *United States v. Stevens,* also nipped in the bud another legislative technique that is extremely dangerous to speech freedoms. The animal cruelty statute had an exceptions clause, stating that it did not prohibit "any depiction that has serious religious, political, scientific, educational, journalistic, historical, or artistic value." The Court said this did not save the law. "*Most* of what we say to one another" does not fall within one of these categories (speech with entertainment value, for example), "but it is still sheltered from government regulation." First Amendment protection "extends to many forms of speech that do not qualify for the serious-value exception." In other words, Congress can't pass a law outlawing whatever kind of speech it disfavors so long as it makes an exception for redeeming social value. That technique would allow Congress to reverse a basic principle of American life: instead of having the right to say whatever we want unless an overriding competing interest requires us to be silent, government would prevent us from speaking unless our particular speech was deemed to be societally valuable.

■   ■   ■

In one case, Jehovah's Witnesses succeeded where a variety of dissidents, socialists, and Communists had failed. Witnesses are conscientious objectors and refuse to do military service. They also urge their adherents and those to whom they preach not to support war, and they did so during World War II. Three Witnesses were convicted under a freshly minted Mississippi law for disseminating literature calculated to encourage disloyalty to the national and state governments and to "create an attitude of stubborn refusal to salute, honor, or respect the flag or government of the United States, or of the State of Mississippi." This was a felony, and they were sentenced to prison for the duration of the war. Their literature said, among other things, that "Satan influences public officials and others to compel little children to indulge in idolatrous practices by bowing down to some image or thing, such as saluting flags . . . which is in direct violation of God's commandment." The evidence also showed that one Witness, in speaking with several women, the sons of two of whom had been killed in battle overseas, offended them by declaring that it was "wrong for our president to send our boys across in uniform to fight our enemies."

On June 14, 1943, in the midst of war, the Court quite summarily ruled that criminal sanctions cannot be imposed for such communications. The Court said no evidence was presented that the Witnesses had done anything "with an evil or sinister purpose," had "advocated or incited subversive action against the nation or state," or had threatened any *clear and present danger* to our institutions." This was the rare case in history in which the clear-and-present-danger test actually resulted in freeing an alleged subversive speaker.

The test originated in Justice Oliver Wendell Holmes's famous opinion in *Schenck v. United States*, the Court's first foray into the subversive speech arena and indeed the Court's first significant decision on free speech under the First Amendment. (As noted in Chapter 1, the 1798 Sedition Act cases never reached the Court before the act expired.) Charles Schenck was convicted under the World War I–Espionage Act, making it a crime to cause "disloyalty" or "insubordination" in the military forces. He had distributed leaflets exhorting men subject to the military draft to assert their rights. The leaflets cited and discussed the Thirteenth Amendment to the Constitution and denounced conscription as slavery. Justice Holmes, for a unanimous Court, ruled against Schenck. He prefaced the ruling by announcing, "The most stringent protection of free speech would not protect a man in falsely shouting fire in a theater and causing a panic." (This vivid metaphor has endured but should never have been applied to a case involving criticism of government policy.)

In the process of deciding *Schenck*, Justice Holmes also announced that the proper test for determining whether allegedly subversive speech could be punished was whether the speaker's words create "a clear and present danger that they will bring about the substantive evils that Congress has a right to prevent." In the same month of March, 1919, Justice Holmes and the Court upheld the conviction of Eugene Debs, the leader of the Socialist Party and five-time candidate for president. Debs was convicted for having made a speech mostly about socialism but including praise for three young men who had refused to register for the draft; he was sentenced to 10 years in prison.

Later the same year, for mysterious reasons, Holmes seems to have changed his mind about this kind of speech and realized how unthreatening it really was, and he wrote an eloquent dissent in *Abrams v. United States*, in which he condemned "persecution for the expression of opinions" and introduced the marketplace-of-ideas concept: "The best test of truth is the power of the thought to get itself accepted in the competition of the market." He said this was the theory of the First Amendment. "It is an experiment, as all life is an experiment. . . . While that experiment is part of our system, I think we should be eternally vigilant against attempts to check the expression of opinions that we loathe and believe to be fraught with death."

As the Court continued to apply Holmes's clear-and-present-danger test and uphold convictions for subversive speech, Holmes continued to dissent (as in Benjamin Gitlow's case discussed in Chapter 1). He also joined Justice Louis Brandeis's magnificent opinion in *Whitney v. California* in 1927, in which Brandeis said the framers believed that "freedom to think as you will and to speak as you think" is indispensable, that "the greatest menace to freedom is an inert people," and that "public discussion is a political duty" of a citizen.

Decades later, during the McCarthy era, the Court upheld the convictions of Communists including Eugene Dennis, finding that their conspiracy to organize the Communist Party and "advocate" overthrowing the United States government satisfied the clear-and-present-danger test. As interpreted in all the subversive speech cases from *Schenck* to *Dennis,* this test was a paper tiger.

While in later cases the Court seems to have abandoned clear and present danger as the standard for deciding whether supposed subversives can be punished for what they write or say, it is striking that only the Jehovah's Witnesses found freedom under it: Schenck, Debs, Gitlow, Whitney, Dennis, and the Communists all lost when the Court applied it.

The Court's willingness to allow government suppression of unpatriotic speech in wartime found a 21st-century friend in

John Yoo, deputy assistant attorney general in the Bush administration. One of Yoo's infamous memoranda, dated October 23, 2001, that supported enhanced presidential power to deal with terrorism within the United States, relied on and quoted Justice Holmes in *Schenck*; Yoo proclaimed for the administration, "First Amendment speech and press rights may also be subordinated to the overriding need to wage war successfully." I prefer President Barack Obama's declaration in his inaugural speech: "Our founding fathers, faced with perils that we can scarcely imagine, drafted a charter to assure the rule of law and the rights of man, a charter expanded by the blood of generations. Those ideals still light the world, and we will not give them up for expedience's sake."

∎　∎　∎

The early Jehovah's Witnesses cases were reaffirmed in the Witnesses' most recent visit to the Supreme Court, in 2002. The town of Stratton, Ohio, enacted an ordinance prohibiting "canvassers" from going door to door to promote any "cause" without obtaining a permit from the mayor's office. Again, the Witnesses did not apply for a permit because they derive their authority to preach from Scripture: "For us to seek a permit from a municipality to preach we feel would almost be an insult to God." But the Court did not confine its decision to protecting the Witnesses' religious freedoms. Harking back to the Jehovah's Witnesses cases from the 1930s and 1940s, Justice John Paul Stevens's opinion for the Court noted that the Witnesses' efforts "to resist speech regulation have not been a struggle for their rights alone" but have benefited "the poorly financed causes of little people" generally. At stake were "door-to-door advocacy" and "anonymous pamphleteering," both vehicles for the dissemination of ideas used by under-funded fringe causes both religious and political. Stevens noted that under the ordinance, "even a spontaneous decision to go across the street and urge a neighbor to vote against the mayor could not lawfully be implemented without first obtaining the mayor's permission." In ringing terms Stevens proclaimed, "It is offensive—not only to the values protected by the First Amendment, but to the very notion of a free society—that in the context of everyday public discourse a citizen must first inform the government of her desire to speak to her neighbors and then obtain a permit to do so."

Again invoking the early Jehovah's Witnesses decisions, the Court concluded: "The rhetoric used in the World War II–era opinions that repeatedly saved [the Witnesses] from petty pros-ecutions reflected the Court's evaluation of the First Amend-ment freedoms that are implicated in this case. The value judgment that then motivated a united democratic people fighting to defend those very freedoms from totalitarian attack is unchanged. It motivates our decision today."

Chief Justice William Rehnquist, alone, dissented. He was sympathetic with the 278-citizen village's lack of sophisticated resources as compared to the 12 Jehovah's Witnesses lawyers in their New York headquarters, and to the village's concern for safety. Rehnquist accepted the village's argument that uncon-trolled door-to-door solicitation could cause not just nuisance but crime. He pointed out that the earlier Witnesses cases had involved *discretionary* permit schemes under which a govern-ment official could grant or deny a permit at his discretion, while the Stratton ordinance was merely a registration requirement, and the mayor had no discretion to deny a permit. But Rehnquist had no answer for Justice Stevens's point that under the law you could not knock on your neighbor's door to ask her to vote against the mayor without first getting a permit from the mayor.

The Jehovah's Witnesses must be considered reluctant First Amendment heroes. Their efforts, while motivated by religion and not by free speech for its own sake, have benefited us all.

· 3 ·

DANNIE MARTIN

"I committed bank robbery and they put me in prison, and that was right. Then I committed journalism and they put me in the hole. And that was wrong." So said Dannie Martin, a convict's convict. A longtime heroin addict and alcoholic, Martin knew jails inside and out, mostly from the insider's point of view. Caught red-handed in a bank robbery in a little town in Washington, Martin was sentenced to 33 years in federal prison.

Prison gave Martin plenty of time to complete the education he never got in the "free" world, and he was an avid reader. He started to write, and it turned out that he had a remarkable gift: the ability to write clearheadedly, honestly, and affectingly about life in prison. No self-pity here, no claims of innocence, no macho braggadocio, no prisoner clichés.

In July, 1986, while in the federal prison at Lompoc, California, Martin mailed off to the *San Francisco Chronicle* an article he wrote on AIDS in prison. It vividly revealed for the public how serious the epidemic was among prisoners. It landed on the desk of Peter Sussman, editor of the *Chronicle*'s Sunday Punch section. Sussman liked the piece, determined to publish it, added Martin's byline, and sent a check for $100 as the standard free-lancer's fee. The article ran on Sunday, August 3, 1986, and readers liked it. Martin continued to submit articles, all first-person essays and vignettes of prison life, and Sussman continued to publish them. They covered diverse facets of prison life that captured the imagination of *Chronicle* readers and made Martin the most popular regular contributor to the Sunday Punch. One of my personal favorites was "Requiem for Mr. Squirrel," a poignant story of how Martin alleviated boredom and the lack of meaningful relationships by feeding a grateful and friendly squirrel, whom the prison officials soon poisoned.

Over the course of about two years, the *Chronicle* published 18 of Martin's articles. His writing won a Scripps Howard Foundation's National Journalism Award and the Society of Professional Journalists' First Amendment Award. One of the articles resulted in freeing a young prisoner who had been improperly sentenced. The San Francisco Board of Supervisors passed a resolution praising Martin because his "unique and eloquent portraits of prison life have won him a large and devoted following in San Francisco."

Federal Bureau of Prisons officials knew of Martin's writing and the fact that he was paid a modest fee for each article, but they did nothing about it. Then, on June 19, 1988, the *Chronicle* published Martin's "The Gulag Mentality," a piece critical of the new Lompoc warden R. H. Rison and his newly instituted policies such as closing down the recreation yard in the morning, confiscating prisoners' personalized chairs, and having guards listen in on counseling sessions with the prison's only psychiatrist. Some prisoners were quoted as being worried about a riot. Martin knew this piece was closer to the edge. But he also knew that the first demand of rioting prisoners is to talk to the press, and his view was that they should not have to wait until *after* the riot to get their complaints heard.

Rison's new policies seemed petty, unnecessary, and designed to make some prisoners unhappy. The article made Rison unhappy. Martin was rounded up by guards and taken to "administrative detention" (known to prisoners as "the hole"). He was charged with violating Bureau of Prisons rules prohibiting a prisoner from conducting "a business" and from receiving compensation "for correspondence with the news media," acting as "a reporter" or publishing under a byline. These regulations had never before been enforced against a prisoner writing for newspapers.

When Rison had Martin locked up after the Gulag article, Martin was able to telephone Sussman (their calls were always recorded by prison officials) and, after Sussman protested to Rison, Martin was released from detention. But he was then promptly transferred to a federal prison in Arizona, far from the environment he had been writing about so well. The prison rules remained the same, a cloud over Martin's ability to continue writing. When Sussman asked Martin if he wanted to continue to write, Martin said, "They can put chains on my body but not on my tongue."

Martin, joined by the *Chronicle*, filed suit against warden Rison. On July 14, 1988 (Bastille Day!), Judge Charles Legge issued an order temporarily stopping the officials from enforcing the Bureau's rules against Martin while the lawsuit was pending. He then wrote another 20 articles for the *Chronicle* while the case worked its way through pretrial proceedings and came to trial. During the trial various prison officials, including Warden Rison and outside experts, testified about the need for the rules in question, and their rationality, or lack thereof. On June 26, 1990, Judge Legge handed down a surprising, confused, and disappointing decision; he ruled against Martin and the *Chronicle* on every point, dissolved the interim order permitting Martin to write, and dismissed the case. However, he granted Martin's application to appeal, finding that the appeal "presents substantial questions."

I represented Martin on the appeal. We argued that the Constitution does not stop at the prison gates, and that prisoners retain at least some First Amendment rights. Clearly, prisoners may be restricted from climbing on mess hall tables and making inflammatory speeches to their brethren about lousy food and mistreatment. But there is no reason why prisoners should not be able to communicate with people *outside* the prison, at least where the officials cannot show that speech restrictions are necessary for prison security.

Martin was still in the Arizona prison when the case came up for argument on August 23, 1991, in the United States Court of Appeals for the Ninth Circuit in San Francisco. I began the argument by noting: "The broad issue before the court is whether the government can effectively prevent publication of prisoner writings by outside mainstream newspapers." I had to concede that restrictions could be imposed where prison security would be threatened but pointed out that the rules in Martin's case applied "regardless of whether there's any effect on prison security." Of the three judges on the panel, two were fairly conservative Republicans, Ferdinand Fernandez and Cynthia Hall.

Judge Fernandez asked, "What about the effect [of a prisoner writing] on the other prisoners? A prisoner says, 'You know, every time that jerk [Martin] publishes something, I lose my Sunday Punch and that just really upsets me; I'm gonna' get that Martin guy.'"

I replied, "That's a fair question, but I think in the balancing that the court must do of the constitutional interests here you ought to find that it's better to black out the handful of prisoners, if any, who read the Sunday Punch than it is to black out the hundreds of thousands of people in the general public who read the *San Francisco Chronicle* and for whom Dannie Martin writes."

The Bureau's rules were incoherent and irrational, and the government lawyer, William C. Brown of the Justice Department, had difficulty defending them. At bottom, he had to persuade the court that a logical connection existed between the Bureau's rules and genuine concern for prison security. Judge Fernandez's questioning of him gave us some cause for optimism. He got Brown to admit that there was no restriction on television or radio interviews of a prisoner, even on a weekly basis. Then the judge followed up: "Why is it such a wonderful [logical] connection if it's in a newspaper and there wouldn't be if it's a weekly radio or weekly television broadcast? The broadcaster comes in and says, 'I'd like to interview you, Mr. Martin. What can you tell us about conditions in the Gulag today?' and Mr. Martin starts reading his article." Similarly, Brown was forced to say that a prisoner was permitted to write a signed letter to the editor every week, but he could not have a byline on any article because this "increases his power within the prison."

Judge Fernandez then zeroed in on whether it made sense

to allow a prisoner to have a byline in the *New Yorker* magazine (not considered the "news media" under the rules) but not in *Time* magazine.

> BROWN: With all due respect to the *New Yorker*, it's a less influential publication.

Brown tried to explain that prisoners "might get mad" at something in a news publication that "normal" people would not get mad at.

> FERNANDEZ: But they wouldn't get mad if it were in the *New Yorker*, only in the newspaper?
>
> BROWN: They had to draw a line somewhere.
>
> FERNANDEZ: Little newspapers are worse than big magazines, correct?
>
> BROWN: News-based publications are worse than non-news publications.
>
> FERNANDEZ: So a very little newspaper circulating in a local area is a bigger danger to the prison than a national magazine which is not a news magazine. Correct?
>
> BROWN (for the fourth time): They had to draw a line somewhere.

After hearing argument, the court took the case under submission, to be decided in due course.

■   ■   ■

I was particularly invested in the issues in Dannie Martin's case because I did the first prisoner First Amendment case actually argued in the United States Supreme Court: *Procunier v. Martinez*, a class action on behalf of all California state prisoners, decided in 1974. The case challenged Department of Corrections rules governing prisoner mail, rules that had been authorized by Director Raymond K. Procunier. The rules made it a disciplinary offense for prisoners in their letters to family to "unduly complain," "magnify grievances," express "inflammatory political, racial, religious, or other views or beliefs," or say anything "defamatory" or "otherwise inappropriate." The evidence showed that officials had censored letters for "criticizing policy, rules, or officials," and for "belittling staff or our judicial system or anything connected with the Department of Corrections." The censors used checklists that, as Director Procunier testified on deposition, allowed them to "fill in the blanks" whenever they thought a letter was inappropriate. The rules were explicitly premised on the proposition that mail is a "privilege," not a "right," that prison officials may grant or withhold in their discretion.

Indeed, until *Martinez*, many courts took a hands-off approach to prisoners' rights cases, deferring completely to the discretion of prison officials and refusing to examine the officials' justifications for denying rights enjoyed by all other citizens. But sometimes, as in *Martinez*, the prisons' policies were so arbitrary and irrational that the courts could not stay their hand. At the argument of *Martinez*, for example, California Deputy Attorney General Eric Collins, a patrician Australian with a plummy accent, urged the Court to find that prisoners had no First Amendment rights: "We wish the right to follow what we [state prison officials] conceive to be correct penological concepts." So he argued that the "underpinning of those First Amendment rights does not exist." The "underpinning" was that the First Amendment is meant to facilitate a "marketplace of ideas" among free people (an echo of Justice Holmes's

Abrams opinion discussed in Chapter 2), and "persons who have been convicted and imprisoned have selected themselves out of a free society." This provoked Justice Thurgood Marshall, a genuine First Amendment hero, to go on the attack:

MARSHALL: When did they [select themselves out], when they committed the crime?

COLLINS: Yes.

MARSHALL: Well he can still write letters, couldn't he? And you couldn't stop him, can you?

COLLINS: Yes.

MARSHALL: You could?! . . . When did the state first get that right to stop him from writing a letter—the moment he is arrested?

COLLINS: . . . When the person is finally imprisoned within this controlled environment . . .

MARSHALL: And the next question is why? . . . It's because he gave it up when he committed the crime?

COLLINS (rattled): No, not. Yes. Yes, that's true.

MARSHALL: He gave up his First Amendment rights when he committed the crime?

COLLINS: He gave up *these* particular First Amendment rights when he committed a crime because the underpinning disappears—

MARSHALL: Did he also give up his right to a trial?

COLLINS: No, Your Honor.

MARSHALL: Well, why do you pick out just one right he loses? Did he give up his right to vote?

COLLINS: No, Your Honor.

MARSHALL: He only gave up his right to write a letter?

COLLINS: Yes, sir.

Other justices were more skeptical about declaring that prisoners had First Amendment freedoms and fearful that we were asking the Court to grant prisoners the full panoply of First Amendment rights. Justice Harry Blackmun, then new to the Court, wanted to be assured that prison officials had the right to *read* prisoner mail (presumably to discover escape plots, drug smuggling, and the like) and asked about other First Amendment rights we were seeking.

I replied, "What we are dealing with here is just expression. It's not obscenity, not libel, not fighting words. We're not talking about conduct; we're not talking about demonstrations, or circulating anything within the prison. Moreover, this is expression contained in letters that are addressed to people who are approved by the Department of Corrections [and on the prisoner's approved correspondent list]."

In other words, we were not seeking a First Amendment charter of liberty for prisoners, only a constitutional minimum—a right not to be punished for criticizing prison officials or saying things that officials might consider otherwise "inappropriate."

The decision in *Martinez* was authored by Justice Lewis Powell for a unanimous court. Clearly chary of opening the courts to a deluge of prisoner complaints, Powell began by noting the traditional "broad hands-off attitude toward problems of prison administration." But hands off means that prisoners have no enforceable rights. Justice Powell declared that this policy of restraint "cannot encompass any failure to take cognizance of valid constitutional claims." And Powell recognized that the California mail rules restricted the rights of *non*prisoners: the prisoners' wives' or mothers' right to read what the prisoners had to say. They hadn't been convicted of anything. The Court had no difficulty in concluding that the rules were not necessary to protect any interest in prison security. Rather, the rules "fairly invited prison officials and employees to apply their own personal prejudices and opinions as standards for prisoner mail censorship. Not surprisingly, some prison officials used the extraordinary latitude for discretion authorized by the regulations to suppress unwelcome criticism." The Court declared the California rules unconstitutional under the First Amendment.

Justice Marshall, joined by other First Amendment heroes, Justices William Brennan and William Douglas, wrote separately to emphasize that a prisoner does not forfeit basic First Amendment rights and is "entitled to use the mails as a medium of free expression not as a privilege, but rather as a constitutionally guaranteed right." Marshall, Brennan, and Douglas went on to conclude that prison officials should not be allowed even to *read* prisoner mail: "A prisoner's free and open expression will surely be restrained by the knowledge that his every word may be read by his jailors and that his message could well find its way into a disciplinary file, be the object of ridicule, or even lead to reprisals." The majority, however, was reluctant to declare that *prisoners* enjoyed rights of free expression and emphasized the rights of the *outside* recipients of prisoner communication.

■   ■   ■

After the argument in Dannie Martin's case had gone well, I was hopeful that the Court of Appeals would follow the lead of *Martinez* and throw out the rules that outlawed Martin's writ-

ing. The Bureau of Prisons must have made a similar assess-
ment, as shortly after the argument and before any decision
came down, Martin was released on parole, and the Bureau's
lawyers then asked the court to dismiss the appeal as "moot."
Since Martin was no longer a prisoner, they said, the prison
rules did not apply to him and he had no standing to ask that
the court rule on hypothetical questions that no longer affected
him. We opposed the government's request, pointing out that
Martin was still subject to unclear parole restrictions and could
summarily be jerked back into prison for a variety of reasons.
But the court, probably relieved that it did not have to decide
knotty questions about whether responsible federal prison
officials had acted unconstitutionally, summarily dismissed
the case as moot. All the expense and effort of trial and appeal
came to nothing.

The outcome reminded me of former bureau director Norman Carlson's testimony at the trial. He testified about the origin of the Bureau's rules. They had been promulgated in 1977
at the same time as the Bureau abandoned its previous prohibition on press interviews of individual prisoners. The Bureau
had vigorously defended that rule, which forbade reporters
from singling out individual prisoners for interviews. Carlson
testified that the purpose of both sets of rules was to muzzle
"anti-establishment" prisoners. He referred specifically to the
Berrigan brothers, Jesuit priests who became federal prisoners
because of their anti–Vietnam War activities. Carlson testified
that "there were a number of inmates in custody who were
extremely anti-establishment . . . and we felt that there was a
need to tighten up to ensure that they did not have access to the
media on a regular basis while they were incarcerated. Again,

we felt that that was one of the punishments that is intended when people are incarcerated."

The *Washington Post* had challenged the no-interview rule in court. Bureau officials testified back then, as they did in Dannie Martin's case, that their rule was necessary to prevent prisoners from becoming media darlings, "big wheels" who could develop their own power base and challenge the authority of the guards. But unbeknownst to the courts struggling to decide the constitutionality of the no-interview restriction, the officials had already determined, *before* the case was decided, to change the rule. Testifying in Martin's case, Carlson said, "We felt that [press interviews] should be a privilege which was extended and not a constitutional right on the part of the inmates, so we purposely waited until that case had gone all the way through the court process before we [abandoned the restriction]." They won that case in the Supreme Court. The restriction was unneeded, but they had made their point, gaining the Court's imprimatur for restrictions on communication from prisons. They pulled off much the same result in Martin's case. Though one may credit Carlson's candor (or naïveté) in confessing the strategy, he earned First Amendment villain status.

When government deceives and manipulates courts, the result is not pretty. And judges are not doing their job unless they are skeptical of government excuses proffered for restricting individual rights. The First Amendment means little if courts simply give government the benefit of the doubt.

After his release Martin continued to write. He collaborated with Peter Sussman on *Committing Journalism*, a compilation of his prison essays connected by Sussman's narrative about

Martin's life and his First Amendment case. (He made only one correction in Sussman's manuscript: he had not "spurned" society's values in his outlaw days; he had "ignored" them.) Sent back to prison five times on parole violations, Martin was in jail when *Committing Journalism* came out. He published a few essays from jail, critical of private for-profit operations ("Private Jailer Reaches out to Gouge Convicts") and of charging prisoners exorbitant fees for basic services such as being booked and visiting the nurse ("Jail Fees a Cruel Twist to 'Paying Your Dues'"). When he was out, Martin also managed to publish two novels, *The Dishwasher* and *In the Hat*. But his unique voice as the wise and observant convict was lost, a loss to the many readers whom he educated, entertained, and provoked, in the best tradition of the First Amendment.

· 4 ·

RAYMOND PROCUNIER
and
ROBERT H. SCHNACKE

Ray Procunier deserved to be considered a First Amendment villain. He authorized and defended the oppressive California prison censorship rules in *Procunier v. Martinez*. But he got a chance to redeem himself, and he rose to the occasion.

The occasion was provided by Robert Schnacke, a federal district judge in San Francisco. Schnacke, like so many judges, was a former prosecutor. While a U.S. Attorney, he had even prosecuted a sedition case in the McCarthy era, charging writer John Powell with having accused the U.S. military of using germ warfare in the Korean War. Schnacke was a crusty, conservative Republican known to be hostile to civil liberties cases. But he had a maverick streak as well, perhaps evidenced by his being caught in a noontime police raid of the Market Street Cinema adult theater in the Tenderloin.

Procunier and Schnacke were two curmudgeonly old-timers who found themselves on opposite sides of a very difficult First Amendment issue: whether prison officials can prohibit news organizations from televising executions. No American execution has ever been televised.

On April 2, 1990, Robert Alton Harris was scheduled to be executed in the gas chamber at San Quentin. He would be the first person to be executed in California in a generation, since 1967, and the news media showed great interest in the event. Capital punishment was then the most decisive issue in California politics, and all candidates for governor and other statewide office had to be "for" it. In 1986, three justices of the California Supreme Court had been voted out of office because the voters perceived that they were frustrating majority will by stalling imposition of the death penalty. When Harris's execution date was announced, virtually every news outlet in the state, national networks, and wire services, wanted to cover it. Warden Daniel Vasquez put out a media advisory stating that 12 media organizations would be allowed to witness the execution.

KQED, the public television station in San Francisco, had been following the political and judicial events relating to the death penalty and, at the time of the Harris announcement, was at work on a documentary on capital punishment. Michael Schwarz, a KQED producer, wrote to warden Vasquez and asked permission to videotape the execution. Vasquez curtly responded that no television equipment would be allowed. Indeed, his newly developed execution protocol provided that news media witnesses would not be permitted to bring any of the tools of their trade—no television cameras, no still cameras, no tape recorders, no sketch pads, no pencils, and no paper. They would have to cover the execution empty-handed.

Schwarz called me and asked whether a prison official can impose those kinds of restrictions on how news organizations cover such an important event. This First Amendment question was not easy. First Amendment protection is at its maximum when government tries to prohibit *publication* of information. But protection of news *gathering* is much more attenuated. The difference is between *speech* and *conduct*: the Supreme Court has always been more suspicious of government restrictions on the content of what a speaker says than of restrictions on the conduct involved in seeking out information for publication. But it was hard to imagine that the warden's restrictions were really required by prison security. I thought they were unjustified. KQED, believing that decisions about how to cover a news event should not be made by the government official involved in the event, decided to sue.

We landed by random selection in Judge Schnacke's court. The Harris execution was stayed, for reasons having nothing to do with our suit, and we had the time to do discovery and inquire into exactly how the execution procedures were set up and the reasons for the restrictions on news reporting. I went up to San Quentin and took the warden's deposition, in which he testified that the reason for prohibiting cameras was to protect the identities of the guards who participated in the execution. We gathered information on how previous executions had been conducted. We also delved into the process by which news media witnesses were selected, learning that this was done by the governor's press secretary, whose main obligation was to ensure favorable coverage of the governor and his policies. And we hired Ray Procunier as an expert witness.

Procunier probably had more experience with prison security issues than anyone in the country. He had been director of the California system for many years. He had worked his way up through the ranks and been warden at several institutions.

After his retirement, he served as director of corrections in Texas, to reform that system after a federal court had found conditions there constitutionally intolerable. He had also run the Virginia and New Mexico systems, consulted on prison issues all over the country, and served as an expert witness in prison litigation for both prisoners and prison officials. He was unimpeachably the kind of person who was *not* a hired gun, and would testify to what he really believed. At the time of the *KQED* case, he was running the state prison in Nevada, called in to straighten things out there.

When I telephoned Procunier (I knew him from the Texas case as well from our earlier encounter in the *Martinez* case), I asked him whether there was any reason television cameras should be excluded from executions. He first said there was: to protect the "dignity" of the proceeding. When I said it seemed to me that was none of a prison official's business, he readily agreed and said he knew of no security reason to limit television coverage. Procunier was a strong supporter of the death penalty, and a no-nonsense prison administrator, but he knew and was willing to testify that whether to televise executions was a political, judicial, or editorial judgment, and televising them would not imperil prison security.

We arranged, over the state's opposition, a court-ordered visit to the gas chamber at San Quentin. Michael Schwarz, Procunier, and I went up there to poke around, test camera angles, and get a sense of how an execution could be televised without interfering with the process or unnecessarily capturing pictures of witnesses or guards who did not want to be on television. We were ready for trial.

■   ■   ■

Five days before the trial was to begin, warden Vasquez announced that he had changed the rules for carrying out executions. *No* reporters would be allowed to witness executions. News crews would not even be allowed on the grounds of San Quentin during an execution. *No* press coverage. The warden's press release said the reason for this new policy was that "the lawsuit forces the warden to elect between forfeiting or retaining control of the prison." It said he was unwilling to "invite" the press if that meant he might have to allow television coverage of the execution. The warden's lawyers—the Attorney General's office—immediately moved to dismiss our case as "moot," arguing that if reporters had no right to be there at all, the court need not decide whether the warden had the right to restrict the tools of the journalist's trade. They were confident that the press had no constitutional right to enter a maximum-security prison to observe an execution; no court had ever so held. So, in addition to the difficult issue of whether prison officials can restrict how news organizations cover the news, we had the blockbuster threshold question—does the press have any First Amendment right of access to government proceedings like executions?

■   ■   ■

The next Monday morning, when Judge Schnacke called the case for trial, he opened court by saying, "We pride ourselves on providing a level playing field for litigants here, but apparently we can't provide a stationary one. I'm not sure what game we're playing or what field we're playing on this morning." But he was not quite willing to let the warden steal the playing field, and he reluctantly agreed to let us put on our evidence and then deal separately with the question of whether the reporters had any right to attend executions at all.

Our strategy at trial was to demonstrate an obvious proposition: a picture is worth a thousand words. We also had to blunt the state's arguments about revealing the identity of guards and other "security" problems.

Michael Schwarz was our first witness. Young, Yale-educated, bright, and a true believer in First Amendment freedoms, he was himself ambivalent about the death penalty, having been the victim of a violent crime. He patiently explained to a skeptical and impatient Judge Schnacke why KQED wanted to videotape the execution and how the use of a television camera contributed materially to the accuracy and completeness of the reporting, adding, "Pictures tell you things that words don't." Schnacke often cut Schwarz off, sometimes cynically questioning his motives and making it clear that the judge believed that the news media could not be trusted and wanted to sensationalize its coverage. For example, he questioned Schwarz on why it was necessary to capture a sound recording as well as video, saying he assumed KQED wanted to record "screams" to make the program more "saleable." Questioning whether the media would really be satisfied with just one camera focused on the condemned man, he asserted that if Schwarz had his "druthers," he would like to have "five cameras in there getting the reaction of all the witnesses and the reaction of the guards and everything else."

This concern with television being an entertainment medium, wanting to capture "reaction" shots, reminded me of the opposition of many judges to televising *trials*. Most judges refuse to allow television in their courtrooms, citing concerns about creating a "circus" atmosphere that will interfere with the ability of jurors to concentrate on the evidence and of witnesses to remember and testify to what happened. But the trial participant most affected by a televised trial is the judge: the judge's behavior is impeccable, fair, and courteous to all, a model of judicial demeanor; the judge never goes to sleep in a televised trial. The deputy attorney general in the *KQED* case often reminded Judge Schnacke that we were not allowed to bring a camera even to the same floor in the federal building, much less into the courtroom, and that it was presumptuous of us to think that we were entitled to take a camera into the heart of a maximum security prison.

Judge Schnacke also brusquely bossed me around. He refused to hear an opening statement about what the evidence would show, and he arbitrarily excluded or limited evidence relevant to how the broadcast technology worked and how KQED would use footage it shot. My then seven-year-old daughter attended the trial for a day and made sketches of the courtroom in a journal along with comments such as "My dad is asking questions," and the judge is "teasing dad." Among other things that the judge "teased" me about was KQED's decision not to videotape an execution over the condemned man's objection. This choice, which we stated at the outset of the case, was based partly on a sense of respect for the person's wish for privacy and partly on not wanting to get sidetracked into litigation with the condemned man. Judge Schnacke ridiculed my willingness to give "veto power" over news coverage to a convicted murderer while denying any such power to the government official responsible for supervising the event.

Our witness George Osterkamp, a very experienced CBS News producer, testified that a television camera could serve as a "neutral witness" at an execution and would enable more complete and accurate coverage. He also emphasized, having done many pieces on world figures and momentous events from the past, how important videotape is for use as a historical record. Judge Schnacke was as sarcastic about Osterkamp's motives as he was of KQED's: "It would be a feather in your cap to have the first live broadcast of an execution . . ."

When we called the great courtroom sketch artist Howard Brodie as a witness, the judge spoke of him with admiration, volunteering that "he got more into one picture than any TV program I've seen in years." Brodie had covered the Watergate trial and testified about sketching many others: "From Chicago conspiracy, Jack Ruby, Manson, Mylai. I can't think of them all. Most of our assassins."

Brodie had witnessed the last execution in California, of Aaron Mitchell in 1967, and his gripping sketches were part of our evidence about the importance of pictures. He also vividly remembered that Mitchell, upon entering the death chamber, screamed, "I am Jesus Christ!" (He had attempted suicide the night before.) Newspaper accounts of the same event either did not mention this or had varying and inconsistent versions (one said he muttered "Oh, my Jesus Christ"), allowing us to argue that sound recording was needed for accurate reporting. The public's reaction to the execution might be different if the condemned man is psychotic as opposed to merely resigned to meet his maker.

Our star expert witness was Ray Procunier. After establishing his qualifications and in light of our being on opposite

sides in the *Martinez* case and in the Texas case, I asked him
whether he had ever "been sued by any of my clients." Procunier answered, "I've been sued by everyone that has a law
degree in California." In many of the lawsuits—an occupa-
tional hazard for prison administrators—he had been represented by Karl Mayer, the same deputy attorney general now
representing the warden in the very case in which Procunier
was testifying.

Procunier's testimony about prison security problems from
using broadcast equipment at an execution was unequivocal:
none. He testified that "prison people historically are guilty of
creating a lot of myths to make our business a lot more important and a lot more romantic than it really is." In his expert
opinion, whether to televise an execution "is not a correctional
decision and . . . it's certainly not a security problem."

On cross-examination by Mayer, he was asked about the
prevalence of prison gangs and whether gang members might
resort to violence if one of their members was executed on
television. Procunier dismissed this possibility, again accusing
prison officials of scare tactics: "[Since televising executions is]
a political or judicial decision, I would hate to see this country
deteriorate to the point where a few gang members would keep
us from making that decision. . . . If you're not careful, [prison
officials will] run a lot of things that's none of their business."

In his cross-examination Mayer also inquired about the possibility of a cameraman hurling the heavy broadcast-quality
camera at the glass in the execution chamber, shattering the
glass, aborting the execution, and perhaps killing the witnesses
in attendance. Amazingly, Judge Schnacke took this seriously
and said: "There may be such a thing in this world as a sui-

cidal cameraman." Procunier thought that this bordered on the "bizarre." In response to the judge's question about how much risk the warden was "obligated to tolerate," he testified that no risk was involved. The camera could be mounted out of reach on a tripod or on one of the pillars in the chamber far from the glass, where it could be operated by remote.

■   ■   ■

Because there had been no executions in California since 1967, Warden Vasquez had no experience at all in conducting one, so his testimony about the potential dangers dreamed up by his lawyers was unlikely to be persuasive. He therefore imported three highly experienced executioners, the wardens from Florida, Georgia, and Texas. The Florida warden testified that if he were required to allow television, he would resign. His position was partly based on his view that "the press doesn't give a damn about the truth." The Georgia warden said he was worried that he could not give his officers complete assurance that they would not be identified when they wanted to remain anonymous, and this too was based on his "mistrust of the media."

The Texas warden, Jack Pursley, was the most experienced in the country, having supervised 38 executions, including one on the day we took his deposition. He testified that prisoner protests might accompany a televised execution. In Texas, some death-row prisoners had started a hunger strike after a recent execution. Asked by the deputy attorney general whether that presents a security problem, Pursley testified it does because "you've got a disgrumbled [sic] group of people that are attempting to buck on you—'buck' is a [Texas] prison term for refusing to work—to prevent themselves from doing their required duties, so consequently, they're a disgrumbled group." His testimony provided an eloquent confirmation of Procunier's testimony about prison officials reaching to find security perils to justify whatever they wish to justify.

I knew Pursley from the Texas case, where he had given me a tour of the death chamber, and I had cross-examined him at length about prison conditions there. He was on the job when Procunier had come in to reform the system, and I asked him whether anyone would have a better grasp of penology than Procunier. It caught Judge Schnacke by surprise when Pursley testified that "with Mr. Turner's help . . . our whole system was turned upside down, and we started over again."

Schnacke asked, "Mr. Turner had a hand in that, too?" When I acknowledged that the warden and I went back a long way, the judge said, "You do get around." Pursley's testimony ended as follows:

TURNER: You've testified in 25 or 30 prison cases, haven't you?

PURSLEY: Yes, sir.

TURNER: And in all of them, you've testified on the side of the prison system, isn't that right?

PURSLEY: Yes, sir. I've always testified on the side of the prison system.

TURNER: And you testified in the Ruiz case, which is the case you've just mentioned?

PURSLEY: '79. Yes, sir.

TURNER: And the prison that you're the warden of was held to be in violation of the federal constitution in that case, isn't that right?

PURSLEY: That is correct.

Warden Vasquez testified that he, like the imported experts, was worried about the camera disclosing the identity of officers working the execution and that someone, some day, somehow, might retaliate against them. Although during Michael Schwarz's testimony we had demonstrated in court ways of obliterating the identifying characteristics of anyone inadvertently caught on camera, Vasquez did not trust this electronic "masking." He also testified that having a camera in the death chamber "would detract from the—whatever solemnness or dignity" of the occasion. To sum up, Vasquez concluded: "The picture in my mind of California wanting to witness—I'm sorry—to film an execution is just—I just can't comprehend it." This was another confirmation of Procunier's view that prison officials will act beyond their purview if you let them.

The testimony about cameras was over, but the big question of whether reporters had any right to attend an execution at all remained unresolved. We asked Judge Schnacke to give us 30 days to develop evidence on this issue, and he agreed to hold the record open.

■   ■   ■

The trial had generated a great deal of media interest, around the country and around the world. I found myself on *Nightline* being quizzed by Ted Koppel, on the *PBS News Hour,* on CNN, on the Spanish equivalent of *60 Minutes,* on radio talk shows, and I was interviewed by Italy's *La Repubblica,* Agence France-Presse, and the U.K.'s *Daily Telegraph.* All the pundits, including George Will, Anthony Lewis, and William Buckley, did columns on the case. The opinions cut across positions on the death penalty. Many death penalty supporters thought televising executions would enhance the deterrent value of capital punishment; others thought it would merely create sympathy for the murderer being killed by the state. Some death penalty opponents supported the suit as confronting the hypocrisy of a barbarian society that wants murderers put to death but wants it done in secret. Others thought the entire prospect was ghoulish and would desensitize the public to the horror of what the state was systematically doing. Some people normally in favor of First Amendment freedoms balked at the idea of televising executions. Prominent First Amendment lawyer Floyd Abrams, predicting the courts' reaction, told me, "They'll treat it like obscenity." (Obscenity has no First Amendment protection, as discussed in Chapter 8.) The *New York Times* columnist and author of two books on the First Amendment, Anthony Lewis, wrote a column acknowledging that we had "a strong argument for letting cameras in." But he argued that we were inviting "a callousness that not even Dickens could imagine" and that the First Amendment does not require "access" to "scenes whose broadcast would further coarsen our society and increase its already dangerous level of insensitivity." Lewis concluded, "We do not need to make executions just another entertainment. We do not need to accept the banality of evil."

■   ■   ■

The "access" issue that Lewis referred to, and the one that Judge Schnacke had to resolve before reaching the cameras issue, emerged relatively recently in American law. Many are surprised that the First Amendment does not operate as a kind of Freedom of Information Act, satisfying the public's right to know. In many other countries, such as Sweden, a major part of the constitution consists of provisions ensuring government transparency and guaranteeing the public and press access to both government proceedings and records. But the Freedom of Information Act was enacted only in 1966. And not until 1980 did the Supreme Court decide that there is any kind of First Amendment right of access, by either press or public, to government facilities, information, or proceedings.

In 1978, I lost a case for KQED in the Supreme Court in which a plurality of the justices held that the press had no right of access, for news-gathering purposes, to a county jail. The Court made it very clear that the First Amendment itself does not guarantee governmental openness, and it emphasized that the press does not have any right of access superior to that of the general public.

In 1980, the Court decided the first in a series of four cases in which it found a First Amendment right of access to certain government proceedings: criminal trials. Two of the cases, in 1984 and 1986, involved death penalty prosecutions. The Court determined that both press and public have a First Amendment right to observe criminal trial proceedings. The Court's analysis had two steps. First, the Court looked to history. Was the proceeding historically open to public and press? If so, this created a presumption of openness. Second, in a practical, real world sense, did openness serve a valid purpose in a democratic society and enhance the integrity of the proceeding itself?

In these cases from the 1980s (the Court has never again considered the access issue and has not ventured beyond criminal trial proceedings), the Court found an unbroken 700-year history of open criminal trials in the Anglo-American judicial system. This satisfied the historical prong of the analysis.

(When I went to Independence Hall in Philadelphia, I noticed that across the hall from the main attraction—the room where the framers wrote the Constitution—is a perfectly preserved 18th-century courtroom. You have to go through a door to enter the room where the constitutional deliberations were held in secret. But on the right, leading into the courtroom, there are three large arches and *no* door at all. Anyone entering the building can see everything in the courtroom and walk in at will. That struck me as an eloquent architectural statement of courtroom openness.)

Having determined that criminal trial proceedings histori-cally were open to public and press, the Court then reasoned that openness served important purposes underlying the trial process itself. It ensured fair trials by discouraging perjury, bias, and misconduct. It educated the public about how a civilized society deals with crime and encouraged public acceptance of the system. And it had a kind of cathartic value, reassuring the public that crime had consequences and justice was being done. The Court determined that these factors all favored openness and concluded that criminal proceedings could not be closed to the public, including the press. These cases from the 1980s provided the framework for our contention that California executions could not be held in secret.

■   ■   ■

We had to do a lot of historical research, rooting around in old case reports, government archives, and newspaper morgues. We learned that California had never had secret executions. Hangings and gassings had not been pretty events, but they had never been concealed from the public. From Gold Rush days until 1858, hangings were carried out in public squares, and a substantial majority of Californians had witnessed them. In 1858, following the lead of eastern states—where the authorities found that public executions were disorderly events frequented by drunkards, hooligans, and pickpockets and concluded that they were teaching lawlessness rather than respect for the law—the California legislature passed an "Act to Abolish Public Executions." From then on, executions would be performed by county sheriffs on jail grounds, but the law guarded against secret executions by requiring the executioner to invite "twelve respectable citizens." The public witnesses would ensure that the execution was in fact carried out, that the right person had been dispatched, and that there was no torture or other mistreatment.

In the first execution after the 1858 law was passed, a San Francisco newspaper reported that "there were, in the prison, as spectators of the execution, about one hundred persons, among whom were ministers, officers, doctors, lawyers, *reporters*, etc." Henry Morse, the condemned prisoner, addressed the crowd as he stepped to the gallows: "I am glad to see so many persons present to witness my execution. I hope it is not idle curiosity that has induced you to come here. I hope this awful example may make a proper impression. I hope you will persuade every one now deviating from the path of rectitude . . . from their sinful ways." Then, said the newspaper, "the miserable man was launched into eternity."

It was evident from newspaper accounts and execution records that crowds, always including reporters, attended all 19th-century executions. In 1891, the Legislature amended the law to provide that executions be performed at Folsom and

San Quentin state prisons rather than by county sheriffs. This amendment changed nothing about public and press access. In 1894, the *San Francisco Examiner* reported that the San Quentin execution of Lee Sing was well attended by the public and press representatives. According to the *Examiner*, Sing said to the assemblage, "Goodbye, all white men," as he stepped "bravely upon the fatal trap." Access by the public and press continued unabated in the 20th century, and some notorious hangings drew large crowds. For a 1936 execution, Earl Warren, then district attorney of Alameda County and later to become Chief Justice of the United States, wrote the warden of San Quentin on behalf of three men who wanted to witness an execution, vouching that "these are all men of integrity and are representative citizens in their communities," and the warden obliged with invitations. For another 1936 execution, the Fresno sheriff got "permission to bring in 14 or 15 very close friends of this office."

In 1937, the Legislature changed the method of execution from hanging to the administration of cyanide gas. All executions were to be performed at San Quentin, where the authorities constructed a gas chamber and a witness area with risers as if they were bleachers at a sports event. At the first lethal gas execution, in 1938, a double execution of Robert Cannon and Albert Kessel (two chairs were equipped in the death chamber), "approximately forty witnesses, including newspaper reporters" attended. Cannon "conversed with spectators and guards until a few moments before a lever, tripped from the outside, sent the cyanide pellets into the acid. The resulting chemical reaction created the deadly fumes which envapored the condemned men." The *San Francisco Examiner* reported "undisguised feelings of revulsion, and frank declarations by prison officials and physicians that hanging is a quicker, more merciful method of execution, and widespread suspicions that the state's new lethal gas chamber is a chamber of horror." Scores of citizen and media witnesses continued to attend all executions. Sixty people witnessed the 1960 execution of Caryl Chessman, which was of course a media extravaganza. "So many people [were] present it seemed like going to a hanging in a public park," reported Mary Crawford of the *San Francisco News-Call Bulletin*. Crawford, the first woman allowed to view a San Quentin execution, was personally invited by Chessman. She wrote: "I'll never see another execution. I think they should invite the legislators who are opposed to the abolition of capital punishment, and let them see for themselves what it's like."

Howard Brodie was one of 58 who witnessed the execution of Aaron Mitchell, who was the last to be executed in California before Harris.

The long, unbroken history showed that the state had not been ashamed of executions. They were not hidden. News reporters had always been able to perform the role envisaged by the First Amendment: to inform the people what the government was doing in their name. So under the Supreme Court cases in the 1980s, there was a presumption that executions should be open to press and public.

The next question was whether openness served any useful purpose. To say that conducting *secret* executions—the kind of practice embraced by totalitarian dictatorships—was a bad and dangerous idea was easy. But the same factors that led the Court to determine that criminal trials should be open also favored open executions. First, openness ensured that executions would be properly conducted, with no torture or other mistreatment. Second, it showed the public the consequences of violent crime and educated people about the culmination of the capital punishment system. Third, it provided cathartic value, giving the public the relief that the ultimate punishment had been imposed.

As Michael Schwarz had testified, many executions had been aired on American television: firing squads from Kuwait and Romania; a beheading in Saudi Arabia; many hangings in Iran, China, Vietnam, and Cuba; simulated but very realistic executions on popular programs such as *L.A. Law,* HBO's *Somebody Has to Shoot the Picture, The Executioner's Song* (about Gary Gilmore's firing squad), and a disgusting film showing both real (foreign) and fake executions called *Faces of Death.* In addition, the assassinations of John and Robert Kennedy and of Lee Harvey Oswald had been shown over and over. The most famous execution of all time, the crucifixion of Jesus Christ, had been realistically portrayed in the movie *The Last Temptation of Christ* (followed more recently by Mel Gibson's *The Passion of the Christ*). But no real American execution had ever been shown. It seemed peculiar that the only executions the people were prevented from seeing were those conducted by their own government in their name.

We bundled up all the historical evidence and presented it to Judge Schnacke, adding the legal arguments based on the Supreme Court's "access" cases, and showed up for a final hearing on June 7, 1991.

■   ■   ■

The judge had heard enough. He did not want to hear any closing argument; he was ready to rule. He put his feet up, leaned
back in his chair, and delivered his judgment—orally. He cited
no cases, engaged in no legal analysis of the complex issues; his
opinion was pure stream of consciousness.

Schnacke began by saying that it was "probably irrational
and unreasonable and capricious to bar the press at this point."
That was basically his ruling on the fundamental "access" issue.
He was deciding, in the most offhanded way and without even
mentioning the First Amendment, that reporters had a right to
witness executions. We breathed a quiet sigh of relief.

Turning to the television issue, Schnacke credited three of
the justifications offered by Warden Vasquez for banning cameras. First, he noted that officers who participate in executions
"frequently want their identities concealed" to protect them
from retaliation by prisoners, or from gangs, "or from any element of the public that is possibly hysterically offended by the
fact of the execution." Schnacke concluded that their identity
"might well be" revealed by a camera and "no rational way"
was available to prevent cameras from intentionally or inadvertently capturing pictures of officers. Schnacke made this ruling
despite the uncontradicted evidence that electronic masking
would prevent identification of anyone and, as he himself ascertained during Michael Schwarz's testimony, the warden would
be able to review the masked videotape before its release. His
ruling did not acknowledge how fanciful the retaliation sce-
nario was or the fact that no officer had ever been retaliated
against, anywhere, in the entire history of capital punishment.

Second, Schnacke referred to the "suicidal cameraperson"
phenomenon, noting that cameras are "heavy objects" that

might create some kind of "threat." Schnacke credited this concern despite his having ascertained from several witnesses that a camera could be bolted down on a pillar or tripod and operated remotely, creating no threat to anything.

Third, Schnacke credited the testimony of the imported wardens that if prisoners themselves were to see a televised execution, it "could spark severe prisoner reaction that might be dangerous to the safety of prison personnel." No evidence supported this as a realistic possibility, and the judge made this ruling despite his having learned from testimony that San Quentin is on a closed-circuit television system that can be shut down by the officials; rather than black out the execution for the prisoners, Schnacke's ruling blacked it out for the general public.

The theme running through Schnacke's "opinion" was that the warden is really not required to trust anybody and that prison officials are the experts. Schnacke asserted that even Ray Procunier would not tolerate any risk in the execution procedure, but Schnacke mischaracterized Procunier's testimony. Procunier had testified, "I don't see that my position would add one jot to the risk of an execution." Procunier's position had been made repeatedly and abundantly clear, as Schnacke well knew: televising executions would present *no* risk to prison security.

Judge Schnacke apparently thought his ruling would not be the last word and would be appealed. As he concluded his opinion, he complimented us for a case well tried and remarked, "I assume they hope this will be merely the first step on their way to achieving their goals, but unfortunately they've stumbled a bit on the first step."

As it happened, neither side appealed. Judge Schnacke issued a permanent injunction prohibiting the warden from excluding the press from executions. The state chose not to appeal this issue, and the injunction is still in effect. KQED, for a variety of reasons, not the least of which was the unrelenting and unfair criticism of its desire to televise executions, chose not to appeal the cameras issue. KQED's CEO said, "We believe that the spirited public debate engendered by the case is in the healthiest tradition of the First Amendment," but that the station had concluded that "[i]t is better not to pursue litigation, but let the public debate on this issue continue in forums other than the court."

■   ■   ■

Judge Schnacke earned First Amendment villain status not simply for ruling erroneously on First Amendment issues, and not simply for taking liberties with the evidence, *knowing* that his rulings were not supported by any persuasive evidence. Rather, his main fault was abdicating the proper judicial role in First Amendment controversies. Every time the government attempts to suppress speech, and the case lands in court, the government claims that competing values require suppression of the speech in question. For example, California argued in Yetta Stromberg's case that waving a red flag would encourage people to want to overthrow the government; the Nixon administration argued that allowing the *New York Times* to publish the "Pentagon Papers" would gravely imperil national security. Contested speech is by definition unpopular and always implicates potential disorder, defiance of authority, and deviation from majoritarian norms. To have free speech, one must tolerate these unsettling qualities. A society that tolerates no risk is not free.

Judges, however, are by nature risk-averse. Their daily duties involve enforcing societal norms. They concern themselves with decorum, order, convention, and rationality. They are part of the government apparatus, have no innate distrust of government officials, and are disposed to give government the benefit of the doubt.

But enforcing the First Amendment requires judges to aim a healthy skepticism at the government's asserted reasons for restricting unpopular speech. Judge Schnacke failed to do that. Judges must hold the government to its burden of proof of establishing that the reasons are not conjectural and in fact are supported by persuasive evidence, that the government's interest in restricting the speech in question really is compelling, and that the interest cannot be served by less restrictive means. Without judges willing to scrutinize officially professed concerns about risk, we will have only orthodoxy, not the First Amendment freedom we claim to want.

■　■　■

When the Supreme Court decided that access to criminal trial proceedings is a First Amendment right, Chief Justice Warren Burger wrote, "People in an open society do not demand infallibility from their institutions, but it is difficult for them to accept what they are prohibited from observing." That is not invariably true. In some instances—such as the death penalty, war, and the slaughterhouses from which our meat comes—people accept the practice *because* they do not see what is happening.

So do I want executions actually to be televised? Certainly not. For many reasons (cost, system fallibility, the inability to distinguish the few first-degree murderers who "deserve" the death penalty from the thousands who do not, and humanitarian concerns), we should not have a death penalty at all. I assume televising executions would be degrading for all, participants and spectators, and I abhor the prospect. But the only thing worse than televising executions is allowing our government both to continue to conduct executions and to prohibit the people from watching them.

· 5 ·

EARL CALDWELL

On June 15, 1969, the *New York Times* carried a story headlined "Black Panthers Serving Youngsters a Diet of Food and Politics." It was an inside view of the Black Panther Party's free breakfast program, and of its revolutionary indoctrination of African American young people in the San Francisco Bay Area. It was full of authentic detail, including the children's repeating after a Panther leader: "I am a revolutionary; I love Huey P. Newton; I love Eldridge Cleaver; I love Bobby Seale; I love being a revolutionary; I feel good; off the pigs; power to the people." An observer was quoted as remarking, "Say anything you want, but there is one unmistakable fact: Black Panthers are feeding more kids every day than anyone else in the whole state of California."

The article was written by Earl Caldwell. It was one of at least 16 *Times* articles Caldwell wrote that year on the Black Panthers. The *Times* had hired Caldwell, an African American, because its white reporters had been unable to get access to the Panthers or establish any rapport with them. The Panthers paid no attention to press credentials or customary reporter-source practices. Caldwell was basically the *Times* emissary to the black radical movement. He had covered riots in several American cities in 1967 and 1968. He was the only reporter actually present at the assassination of Martin Luther King Jr. in Memphis and wrote the *Times*'s front-page story on it. Caldwell developed relationships with Panther sources and was the only reporter in the *Times* organization able to do so.

Caldwell reported on the Panthers virtually from the inception of the party in 1966, and his illuminating stories contributed markedly to the public's understanding of the Panthers. In addition to observing Panther activities firsthand, he was able to get revealing on-the-record quotes from Panthers. One story, for example, in the *Times* on September 6, 1968, quoted a Panther about how the police control the black community with force: "Their power is on their hips. Take those guns away from those pigs and they are nobodies. The only way to counteract this power is with a gun in your hand." When asked what white sympathizers could do, the Panther responded, "Give us some money and give us some guns."

Attorney General John Mitchell determined that the Black Panther Party was a "threat to national security," and FBI Director J. Edgar Hoover testified before a House committee that the FBI was intensifying its efforts to penetrate the Panthers by informants. In the few days from December 23, 1969, to January 12, 1970, FBI agents visited Caldwell six times and attempted to interview him. They wanted to set up regular meetings with him. He refused, knowing that if the Panthers learned that he had any conversation whatever with the FBI, he would lose all access to them. One day, Caldwell recalled later in a *Frontline* interview, an agent left a message at his office:

"Tell Earl Caldwell we're not playing with him. He doesn't want to tell it to us, he doesn't want to talk to us, he can tell it in court." The following Monday, they came back with a subpoena for him to appear before a federal grand jury, and they wanted all of his notebooks, tape recordings, and anything else he had accumulated over a period of about 16 months of reporting on the Black Panthers. Caldwell noted that the subpoena "didn't mention the *New York Times* at all. It was just Earl Caldwell, the reporter. Very vulnerable."

Caldwell was afraid even to go to the federal courthouse in San Francisco and appear before the grand jury, much less testify. He was certain that doing so would make it impossible to continue reporting on the Panthers and other dissident groups. Grand jury proceedings are secret, attended only by the prosecutor and the jurors themselves, and outsiders have no way to know whether a witness cooperated, or what he said. Caldwell had to fight the subpoena. Through black journalist friends, he was able to arrange a late-night meeting in Palo Alto with Professor Anthony Amsterdam, then at Stanford, who was a legendary figure in the legal civil rights movement. Amsterdam quickly sized up the situation and agreed to represent Caldwell. Amsterdam had a long relationship with the NAACP Legal Defense & Educational Fund, Inc., where I then worked, and I helped Amsterdam on Caldwell's case.

On March 17, 1970, Caldwell moved to quash the subpoena. The motion alleged that "compelling Mr. Caldwell's appearance before the grand jury will cause grave, widespread and irreparable injury to [First Amendment] freedoms of the press, of speech and of association; and this Court should not permit a use of its process that so jeopardizes vital constitutional interests in the absence of an overriding governmental interest—not shown here—in securing Mr. Caldwell's testimony before the grand jury." The motion was accompanied by an impressive collection of affidavits. Caldwell's own stated: "If I am forced to appear in secret grand jury proceedings, my appearance alone would be interpreted by the Black Panthers and other dissident groups as a possible disclosure of confidences and trust and would similarly destroy my effectiveness as a newspaperman." Backing this up were affidavits from journalism titans Walter Cronkite, Eric Sevareid, Mike Wallace, Dan Rather, and others. These testified to several basic points: that confidential communications to reporters are "indispensable" to gathering the news; that when reporters are subpoenaed, their confidential sources are terrified of disclosure and "shut up"; that the mere appearance of a reporter in secret grand jury proceedings, where what he says cannot be known, "destroys his credibility, ruptures his confidential associations," and damages his ability to function professionally; and that subpoenas to reporters end up "critically impairing the news-gathering capacities of the media and impoverishing the fund of public information and understanding." Cronkite, for example, testified by affidavit that he depended "constantly on information, ideas, leads, and opinions received in confidence." He further stated, "Such material is essential in digging out newsworthy facts and, equally important, in assessing the importance and analyzing the significance of public events. Without such materials, I would be able to do little more than broadcast press releases and public statements."

Caldwell's motion did not claim that he had an absolute

right to avoid appearing before the grand jury. Rather, it contended that he could not be forced to appear unless and until the government had shown that he in fact had information relevant to a crime being investigated by the grand jury, that the information was not available from other sources, and that the need for the information outweighed the damage to his ability to function as a reporter. As a precaution, Caldwell put some notes and other materials, including materials about the King assassination, in an old plastic airline flight bag and brought it to our Legal Defense Fund office, where the materials would be better insulated from government demands.

Federal district judge Alfonso Zirpoli (one of the lower court judges who invalidated the prison censorship rules in *Procunier v. Martinez* in Chapter 4, and ordinarily a First Amendment hero) tried to split the baby. He refused to quash the subpoena. He required Caldwell to appear before the grand jury, but he granted a protective order saying that Caldwell "need not reveal confidential associations" that impinge on his ability to gather news until "a compelling and overriding national interest" was established by the government.

Caldwell rejected Judge Zirpoli's attempted compromise and refused to appear before the grand jury. He went to the judge's courtroom, repeated his refusal before the judge, and restated his constitutional objections. The court overruled the objections and held Caldwell in contempt. Judge Zirpoli stayed his contempt order, permitting Caldwell to appeal. The Ninth Circuit Court of Appeals went further than Judge Zirpoli had been willing to go. Agreeing with us that Caldwell should not have to appear unless the government had shown a compelling need, it vacated the contempt order. The Nixon administration Justice Department took the case to the Supreme Court.

■   ■   ■

The years leading up to and around Watergate saw a noticeable increase in investigative reporting. Journalists did not simply attend public events and summarize government or corporate reports but began to *dig* into places, documents, and conversations that otherwise would remain secret. When "Deep Throat" whispered to Woodward and Bernstein secrets about the Nixon administration and the activities that sent John Mitchell and many others to jail, he did so under assurances of confidentiality: that his name would not be disclosed by the reporters or the *Washington Post*. Reporters around the country learned to say to reluctant sources, "Don't worry, we won't use your name, and we'll never disclose who told us this." Sometimes that was necessary to persuade the source to tell what he knew, and without the promise of confidentiality, the information would not become public.

In Louisville, Kentucky, Paul Branzburg, a reporter for the Louisville *Courier-Journal*, wrote revealing stories about a marijuana and hashish ring. He was subpoenaed to a grand jury to testify about the crimes he saw and heard. Branzburg appeared but refused to testify and was held in contempt. In Massachusetts, Paul Pappas, a television reporter covering civil disorders in New Bedford, was allowed into the local Black Panther Party headquarters for an anticipated police raid in return for his promise not to disclose anything he observed except the raid, which didn't materialize. Pappas didn't write any story, but the authorities apparently learned of his Panthers connection and he was subpoenaed to a grand jury. He refused to answer questions and was held in contempt. The *Branzburg* and *Pappas* cases went to the Supreme Court about the same time as Caldwell's case.

The Supreme Court consolidated all three cases, heard argument, and decided them together under the name of *Branzburg v. Hayes*, in 1972. It was the first time—and the *only* time—that the Court decided whether reporters have a First Amendment right not to disclose confidential sources and information. While battles continue to rage over reporters' "shield" issues (protecting confidential source material from compelled government inquiry), and journalists such as former *New York Times* reporter Judith Miller have gone to jail, the Court has not revisited the question.

■   ■   ■

Lurking in the background of the *Caldwell* case and any other reporter's shield case are two larger First Amendment questions that are well worth pondering: whether reporters should have rights that ordinary citizens do not have, and whether the explicit mention of "the press" in the First Amendment, singling it out for protection in addition to the freedom of "speech," means anything.

Ordinary citizens—you and I—who are served with grand jury subpoenas do not have any "privilege" not to appear and testify to what we have seen or heard. The assumption of our system is that a grand jury investigating crime is entitled to everyone's testimony. To be sure, well-recognized evidentiary privileges protect confidences between attorneys and clients, husbands and wives, and doctors and patients. And the Fifth

Amendment protects against being compelled to give incrimi-
nating testimony about oneself. But the reporters in the *Branzburg* case were seeking a right that the rest of us do not have:
the right not to be required to disclose information received in
confidence from a news source. This assertion of "press exceptionalism" presents a difficult issue of public policy as well as
a constitutional question never addressed before *Branzburg*.

The even broader question is whether the words "or of the
press" in the First Amendment add anything of substance to the
"freedom of speech." The "press" is the only nongovernmental
entity even mentioned in the Constitution. (The document
has not a word about corporations, schools, political parties,
or many other institutions basic to our society.) The question
is whether this explicit recognition of the press confers on it
rights beyond those protected for all of us by the free-speech
clause, whether the press has some kind of preferred position
under the First Amendment.

■   ■   ■

The decision in Earl Caldwell's case dealt a severe blow to the
notion that the press has any such preferred position. The opinion in *Branzburg v. Hayes* was written by Justice Byron White,
no First Amendment hero. It was a squeaker of a decision, 5–4,
ruling that reporters do not have a First Amendment right not
to appear before a grand jury and testify about confidential
sources or information.

Justice White began by acknowledging that the First
Amendment must provide *some* protection for news *gathering* in addition to publication: "Without some protection for
seeking out the news, freedom of the press could be eviscer-

ated." But he pointed out that the use of confidential sources was not forbidden, and the government was not attempting to force the press to publish its sources. Rather, White said, "The sole issue before us is the obligation of reporters to respond to grand jury subpoenas as other citizens do." White went on to point out that the First Amendment does not invalidate every measure that might burden the press or make it more costly or difficult to report the news. For example, the press, like all businesses, must comply with laws of general applicability like the labor, minimum wage, and tax laws: news organizations have to bargain with unions, pay the minimum wage, and pay their taxes just as other businesses do, even though these laws impose burdens and handicap to some degree the ability to gather and publish the news.

As for Cronkite's and other journalists' contentions that sources would "dry up" if reporters could be forced to disclose them, White was skeptical to the point of cynicism. He was just not persuaded that this would happen. After all, he noted, no one had ever invoked a journalist's privilege not to testify for 180 years of First Amendment history, yet the press had "flourished." Nor did he think such a privilege would be good public policy: the needs of law enforcement to obtain all relevant testimony outweighed what he viewed as the speculative impact on a reporter's news-gathering ability. Paul Branzburg had actually witnessed crimes, while Caldwell and Pappas had not, but the Court made nothing of that distinction.

Rejecting the idea of a reporter's privilege, White also noted the practical problems that would have to be resolved if such a privilege were recognized, principally defining *who* would be permitted to claim the privilege. White said the "liberty of the press is the right of the lonely pamphleteer" as much as it is of "the large metropolitan publisher," and that it is a "fundamental personal right" not confined to newspapers and periodicals. White said establishing some kind of reporter's privilege is a task suited for a legislature, not the Court, and invited Congress and the states, if they believed journalists should have some protection, to enact laws defining who is protected and the scope of the protection.

Justice Lewis Powell provided the crucial fifth vote and wrote a brief concurring opinion straddling the fence. He said that if a subpoena "implicated confidential source relationships without a legitimate need of law enforcement," a judge should quash the subpoena. He added that, on a case-by-case basis, the judge should seek the proper balance "between freedom of the press and the obligation of all citizens to give relevant testimony."

Justice Potter Stewart dissented, complaining that the majority's "crabbed view" of the First Amendment invited law enforcement to "annex the journalism profession as an investigative arm of government." He argued that the right to publish news was unquestioned and that a "corollary" must be the right to *gather* news. So far, so good. Then he concluded: "The right to gather news implies, in turn, a right to a confidential relationship between a reporter and his sources." But this conclusion—something of a logical leap—depends on accepting as fact Cronkite's and other journalists' testimony about the need to assure confidentiality and sources drying up without such assurance, and the majority was unwilling to give that testimony dispositive weight.

(To bolster his argument on the right to gather news, Stewart quoted James Madison: "A popular government, without popular information, or the means of acquiring it, is but a prologue to a farce or a tragedy; or, perhaps both." Well said, but out of context; Madison was speaking about the need for *education*, not the press.)

■   ■   ■

In 1974, not long after participating in the Court's *Branzburg* decision, Justice Stewart went up to Yale and gave a speech entitled "Or of the Press." It was provocative. Stewart argued that the primary purpose of the press clause was to recognize what was essentially a fourth branch of government, the "established press," that would provide "organized, expert scrutiny of government." The press would be autonomous, independent, and an adversarial check on the three official branches. He argued that the press clause was thus a "structural" provision. Stewart contended that if freedom of the press protected only expression, it was redundant of the freedom of speech that we all have. Stewart stopped short of advocating any specific advantages his position conferred on the press. And he pointedly said the press clause does not operate as a "Freedom of Information Act," requiring the government to give the press information it seeks.

Not everyone agrees with Stewart. Notably, Anthony Lewis, the *New York Times* columnist and First Amendment scholar, ridiculed Stewart's speech. Lewis pointed out that the framers were as concerned about protecting books and pamphlets as they were about protecting newspapers. He also noted that the Supreme Court has *never* based a decision on the press clause. Even the great decisions protecting the press, such as the *Pentagon Papers* case, which protected against "prior restraints" (prepublication government censorship), and *New York Times v. Sullivan*, which protected against libel suits by public officials, did not rely on the press clause at all; and the Court's reasoning in *Sullivan* was that we *all* have the right to criticize government. (In its 2010 *Citizens United* decision, the Court said, "We have consistently rejected the proposition that the institutional press has any constitutional privilege beyond that of other speakers." On the other hand, the Court has never ruled that the press clause has *no* independent significance.)

Further, Lewis argued that giving the press special rights would be bad public policy. It would add to the public's perception that the press is arrogant and unaccountable and lead to attempts to *make* it accountable (perhaps treating the press as a public utility, required to carry whatever communications people wanted published, or required to ensure publication not just of the editor's choice of news and opinion but of views representative of the community). Finally, Lewis noted the difficulty of defining who *is* the press. Stewart referred vaguely to the "established" press. But why should freelancers, academic authors, and now bloggers be excluded? Traditionally, the "lonely pamphleteer" has been considered to have the same First Amendment rights as the editor of the *New York Times*. As Lewis noted, if the definition of the "press" is broadened to include communicators of all kinds, Stewart's thesis enshrining the "established" press as a structurally protected entity loses its point. Lewis concluded that by adding the press clause, the only goal of the framers (whose true intent on this point will never be known, as there is precious little legislative history of it) must have been to ensure constitutional protection for the printed as well as the spoken word (hence "speech" and "press").

My own view is that the framers, as evidenced in part by James Madison's eloquent tribute to the press in his famous report on the Virginia Resolutions on the Sedition Act of 1798, meant the press to have some special status. Madison said, "To the press alone, chequered as it is with abuses, the world is indebted for all the triumphs which have been gained by reason and humanity over error and oppression." He added that without the press stirring the citizenry against the British crown, we might still be colonies. I find it hard to believe that the framers wrote the press clause as just another way of protecting the same freedom of expression that we all have. Perhaps the framers singled out the press for special mention because printers and publishers in England and the colonies had more often been subjected to official restraints like licensing, censorship, and prosecutions for seditious libel.

This is an interesting theoretical debate, but its resolution in the real world has largely been limited to only two issues. One is the *Branzburg-Caldwell* issue, whether reporters, because they are reporters, have the right not to be forced to disclose confidential information. The other is whether reporters have a right of access to government places or information, a right not enjoyed by the general public. The general rule is that reporters have no right to go where other citizens have no right to go. For example, reporters are not exempt from trespass laws and are not allowed to enter private property even in hot pursuit of a major story. But denying press access to government facilities and documents means that the public will never receive some information about what their government is really up to (see

Chapter 6). Without a First Amendment right of access, or a much beefed-up Freedom of Information Act, an administration as secretive as the last Bush administration can conceal a great deal of information that citizens in a democracy ought to have.

■   ■   ■

The disappointing decision in Earl Caldwell's case was not the end of the story. The decision did not sit well with the "established press" or, indeed, with writers of all kinds. Many seized on what Justice Stewart called Justice Powell's "enigmatic" opinion and invoked his reasoning to continue to urge courts to quash or limit subpoenas. They had some success in lower courts, especially in civil cases in which reporters were dragged into someone else's litigation and asked to spill the beans about information obtained in confidence. They also had considerable success in convincing *states* to adopt "reporters' shield" laws, either legislatively or by court decision. In California, for example, shortly after *Branzburg,* the Newspaper Publishers Association got the legislature to enact a strong law that prohibited holding a reporter (defined essentially as someone working for mainstream news media) in contempt for refusing to reveal not only confidential sources and information but also "any unpublished information" (i.e., any information that the reporter chose not to put in the story). A virtually identical provision was added by the voters to California's state constitution in 1980. In all, 31 state legislatures have enacted shield laws and another 18 states have adopted similar protections by court decision, leaving only Wyoming without any protection for reporters.

But the Congress did not act. Without any federal protection, reporters like the *Times*'s Judith Miller landed in jail. Whatever one may think about her reporting on Iraq's weaponry or her relationship with Scooter Libby, she went to jail solely because she refused to reveal communications with her source to the federal grand jury. Others, including the *Times*'s James Risen, who used confidential whistleblower sources to break the story of illegal wiretapping of United States citizens by the National Security Agency (NSA), were threatened with prosecution. Without a federal law, reporters are put in the uncomfortable position of being able to protect sources if they happen to be subpoenaed by a state grand jury but of having to burn the sources if it's a federal grand jury; this leaves them unable to give their sources promises they can rely on.

Congress has finally drafted a bipartisan law, the Free Flow of Information Act, that would provide significant protection for reporters, probably including bloggers, historians, and book authors. President George W. Bush's threatened veto previously stalled the bill, but President Obama cosponsored an earlier bill while he was still a senator and said during the presidential campaign that he favored its reporter protections. As of this writing, the bill has passed the House and is pending in the Senate. Surprisingly, the Obama administration weighed in with last-minute national security objections, but some bill seems likely to pass. Almost four decades have elapsed, but now perhaps Earl Caldwell's position will be vindicated.

■   ■   ■

Having urged the necessity and urgency of obtaining Caldwell's testimony about the Black Panther Party's operations

and plans, claiming that law enforcement needs clearly outweighed the fact that his ability to report on the Panthers
would be destroyed, the government mysteriously seemed
to lose interest in the case. After the case was remanded by
the Supreme Court to Judge Zirpoli's court, the government
prosecutors allowed the grand jury term to expire without
again attempting to require Caldwell to appear and testify.
By then the Watergate story dominated the news, and the Justice Department apparently did not want to pick another fight
with the press. Also, as Earl Caldwell later told me, by then
most of the Panther leaders were either out of the country
or "in the cemetery," and the party he had covered "virtually
didn't exist anymore." The government had successfully gotten
the Supreme Court ruling it wanted, and it had put an end to
Caldwell's Panther reporting.

Some time after the decision, Caldwell called and asked if
we still had the bag of his notes and materials that he had left
with us for safekeeping. I retrieved the bag from the back of a
closet, and he came and picked it up. The government never
saw the materials and never got the testimony that it claimed
was so essential. The Republic still stands.

Hostile reaction to the Supreme Court's *Citizens United* corporate speech decision   *Source:* Andy Turner

Yetta Stromberg while out on bail pending her appeal to the Supreme Court, 1931
Source: Corbis

Jehovah's Witnesses proselytize door to door in Oakland *Source: San Francisco Chronicle*

Dannie Martin and Peter Sussman editing an article during Martin's First Amendment trial *Source: San Francisco Chronicle*

(above left) Raymond Procunier as director of California prison system   *Source:* California Department of Corrections and Rehabilitation
(above right) United States District Judge Robert Schnacke
Source: United States District Court, Northern District of California

Howard Brodie
sketch of the
1967 execution
of Aaron Mitchell
Source: Howard Brodie

Earl Caldwell testifying before House Judiciary subcommittee on need for reporters' protection, after Supreme Court ruling, 1973 *Source: Corbis*

Richard Hongisto as he was portrayed on cover of *San Francisco Bay Times*. *Source: San Francisco Bay Times*

Ku Klux Klan leader Clarence Brandenburg

Source: Cincinnati Enquirer

Larry Flynt with the *Hustler* ad parody of Rev. Jerry Falwell, 1988

Source: Corbis

Clinton Fein, First Amendment true believer and digital artist

Source: Trace Cohen, courtesy of Clinton Fein

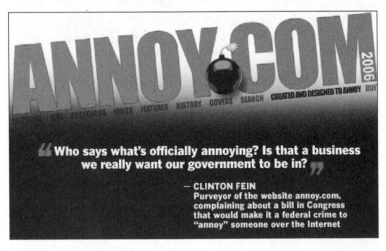

ANNOY.COM 2006
CREATED AND DESIGNED TO ANNOY BUY

"Who says what's officially annoying? Is that a business we really want our government to be in?"

— CLINTON FEIN
Purveyor of the website annoy.com, complaining about a bill in Congress that would make it a federal crime to "annoy" someone over the Internet

Annoy.com home page   *Source:* Clinton Fein

· 6 ·

RICHARD HONGISTO

Richard Hongisto was an enigma: a maverick cop who became a politician, a jailer who became a First Amendment hero, a police chief who became a First Amendment villain. He helped in trying to open the doors of government. Later he acted like a petty tyrant and clumsily tried to suppress criticism that stung him. He lurched from friend of a free press to destroyer of newspapers.

Hongisto worked as a San Francisco police officer in the turbulent 1960s. He was the only white officer to testify in federal court on behalf of the plaintiffs in a lawsuit alleging discrimination against African Americans on the police force. In 1971, he ran for Sheriff against the longtime incumbent and won an upset victory. As sheriff, he recruited minority deputies, appointed the first openly gay deputy, and tried to improve jail conditions. In charge of the San Francisco jails, he opened the doors to the press. In 1972, for example, he allowed local public television station KQED to do a 90-minute *live* television program from inside the jail. It vividly showed squalid jail conditions and included on-the-spot interviews with both prisoners and guards.

■ ■ ■

In 1974, state and federal prison officials won a case in the U.S. Supreme Court, *Pell v. Procunier.* The Court upheld prison rules prohibiting the press from singling out individual prisoners for interviews. The rationale of the prohibition was to prevent prisoners from using the media to become "big wheels," who could build their own power base by commanding attention inside and out and threaten the officials' control of the prisons. The rule in California had been inspired by trying to contain charismatic prisoners like George Jackson and other militants, whom journalists like Eve Pell wished to interview.

The close 5–4 decision in *Pell* was written by Justice Potter Stewart. He emphasized that the press had reasonably good access to prisons like San Quentin; reporters were able to enter, look around, bring cameras, and interview randomly encountered prisoners. The only restriction was the no-interview-of-specific-prisoners rule. Stewart said no attempt was made to conceal prison conditions and found the officials' concern about celebrity prisoners to be reasonable. He wrote: "Newsmen have no constitutional right of access to prisons beyond that afforded the general public [and no] special access to information not shared by members of the public generally."

Justice Lewis Powell, a recent appointee of President Richard Nixon, surprisingly dissented. In Powell's view, the press acts as the "eyes and ears" of the public, who can't go to prisons and check out conditions and depend on reporters to inform them about what is going on in these taxpayer-supported institutions. Powell reasoned that the blunderbuss rule prohibiting *all* specific prisoner interviews was too broad, and a narrower rule limiting interviews in individual cases in which there was actual danger to prison security would be more consistent with the First Amendment.

Justice Stewart's majority opinion contained two significant ambiguities, perhaps reflective of his own ambivalence about the role of the press. First, it was unclear whether the result turned on the fact that the press had good access to the prisons in question, and therefore the no-interview restriction was inconsequential, or whether the press in fact had no constitutional right of access to prisons at all, and therefore had to accept whatever access the officials chose to give. Second, it was unclear whether the result turned on the fact that the press was seeking *special* access not available to the general public, or whether *neither* press nor public has any First Amendment right to enter and observe a prison.

■　　■　　■

Less than a year after the *Pell* decision, I received a call from Mel Wax, the news director at KQED and the anchor of its then daily news program. KQED had been following stories about the Alameda County jail at Santa Rita. In 1972, a federal judge had found conditions there "shocking and debasing" and a violation of the Eighth Amendment's ban on cruel and unusual punishment. In March, 1975, KQED's *Newsroom* program reported on the suicide of a prisoner in the maximum-security part of the jail previously condemned by the federal judge. KQED also reported statements by a jail psychiatrist that the oppressive conditions were partly responsible for prisoners' mental problems. The psychiatrist was fired after he appeared on the news program.

Wax told me that he had just called the sheriff of Alameda County, Tom Houchins, and asked permission to send a reporter and cameraperson to the jail. Houchins responded that his policy was *no* press access to the jail. None. Wax asked me if under the First Amendment the sheriff's no-press policy was constitutional. I was familiar with the *Pell* decision and with its ambiguities. I told Wax that completely barring the press seemed unreasonable, at least where there was no risk to jail security. Wax decided to sue the sheriff. I decided to call Dick Hongisto. We brought a civil rights action for KQED in federal court in San Francisco.

■　■　■

Hongisto promised to be an ideal expert witness: a seasoned law enforcement officer and an articulate and intelligent jailer who had a completely open door for the press. He could, and did, testify that allowing reporters to pursue stories in the jail caused no security problems and actually helped him as sheriff to garner public and taxpayer support for improving conditions. He testified before Judge Oliver Carter about having permitted the live KQED broadcast from the jail. Asked whether any security problems were caused, he said, "None whatsoever." He volunteered, "I've routinely, many times, had reporters stay in our institution overnight." On "many, many" occasions, he testified, he had allowed television, radio, and newspaper reporters—and judges too—in the four jails that he was in charge of, without any disruption of jail routine or risk to security. He also testified that closed institutions like jails and prisons "routinely end up being places that are extraordinarily abusive to people," and exposing conditions, through the press, motivated county supervisors to meet their responsibilities to provide adequate funding.

Judge Carter heard testimony from Hongisto, Sheriff Houchins, and several other witnesses at a hearing on our motion for a preliminary injunction. We sought an order that would require Houchins to allow KQED and other press representatives to enter the Santa Rita jail to cover the news. Conscious of Justice Stewart's "no greater access" statement in *Pell*, I made the fateful decision to join as plaintiffs in the case two local chapters of the NAACP. Their members were representative of the general public who were concerned about how their tax dollars were being spent and whether a new jail was needed; and they depended on the press to inform them about conditions there. The idea was that *both* press and public were seeking access to what was going on in the jail. My idea backfired, but not until the case reached the U.S. Supreme Court.

Sheriff Houchins's lawyer was career county counsel Kelvin Booty. He, too, had read *Pell*, and the defense was that the sheriff would provide the press with precisely the same access as the general public. Before we sued, that was no access. When we sued, the Sheriff initiated a series of six monthly guided tours of Santa Rita. The tours were open to both press and public, on an equal basis. The first tour was conducted, inadvertently I am sure, on Bastille Day, July 14, 1975. It was oversubscribed, as was the entire series of tours that year, almost immediately. People on the tour were not allowed to bring cameras or recording equipment, or to talk to any prisoners. Indeed, the prisoners were hustled out of sight during the tours, so what the tourists saw was basically architecture. The antiseptic tours did not include the maximum-security part of the jail where most of the problems had arisen. And, of course, having tours on a monthly, scheduled basis gave the press no chance to report on any breaking news event. Sheriff Houchins's position was consistent to a fault: the press had no greater right of access to his jail than the general public.

Judge Carter, doubtless reassured by Dick Hongisto's helpful testimony that press access presented no security problems, rejected Sheriff Houchins's doctrinaire stance. He issued a preliminary injunction requiring Houchins to allow press access "at reasonable times and on reasonable notice" except when a genuine security emergency might arise. Reporters could use cameras and recording equipment and could interview randomly encountered prisoners. This arrangement seemed like a reasonable accommodation of the competing values: satisfying the interest of both the press and the public in jail conditions, and ensuring the Sheriff's need for jail security.

To my surprise, the Sheriff appealed. The Court of Appeals granted a stay of Judge Carter's order. We asked that the appeal be expedited so that the case would not languish on the court's docket for years. The court heard argument and unanimously ruled in KQED's favor. Unfortunately, the three judges on the appellate panel could not agree on a single theory for why the First Amendment required access of the kind ordered by Judge Carter. They seemed to be baffled by the *Pell* ambiguities and unsure how far they could go in recognizing a brand new First Amendment right: a right of access to government facilities and information.

Again to my surprise, the Sheriff petitioned the Supreme Court for review. Justice William Rehnquist granted a stay of our injunction. The case was set for argument before a shorthanded court. Justices Thurgood Marshall and Harry Blackmun did not sit on the case. Marshall recused himself because the NAACP parties were in the case. Having been general counsel for the national NAACP back in the 1930s and 1940s, Marshall routinely recused himself in cases in which NAACP parties appeared, however tangentially. My decision to include the NAACP chapters to demonstrate that both the public and the press supported access had lost us what was almost certainly a crucial vote. How Justice Blackmun would lean at this stage in his tenure on the Court could not be known. He did not participate because he had prostate surgery shortly before the argument.

■   ■   ■

At stake in the argument of *Houchins v. KQED* was a quite fundamental First Amendment issue that the Court had never been asked to resolve: whether there was any such thing as a First Amendment right of access. Counting heads on the Court, I thought we would certainly get Justice William Brennan's vote; he was always a First Amendment stalwart. I was hopeful, based on his dissent in *Pell*, that Justice Powell might go along. Justice John Paul Stevens, President Gerald Ford's only appointee to the Court, was new and had no track record on First Amendment issues. But as a court of appeals judge, he had seemed appropriately skeptical of prison officials' excuses for denying prisoners' rights, and he seemed persuadable. On the other hand, Chief Justice Warren Burger had never been friendly to press arguments, seemed mistrustful of the press, and virtually always gave the government the benefit of the doubt. William Rehnquist was very conservative and had not yet given any hint of interest in First Amendment freedoms. Byron White was nominally a Democrat and had been appointed by President John F. Kennedy but had always been suspicious of press claims, as exhibited by his *Branzburg* opinion. That left Potter Stewart as the man in the middle. He was the author of *Pell* and the "Or of the Press" speech, he was frequently a swing vote on the Court, and the case could not be won without him.

Kelvin Booty argued first for the Sheriff. Early on, Justice Stevens asked Booty whether he contended that "the whole problem could be solved by having zero access to public and press both." Booty answered that he did not. My heart sank when Stewart interjected, "Why don't you? It's a perfectly logical position to take." Booty responded, "Yes, it is a logical position, Your Honors, but it isn't our position. . . . I'm not convinced, and, considering the body that I'm speaking to, I'm not convinced that that's what the Court held in *Pell*." Stewart's rejoinder seemed surreal: "What the Court held in *Pell* was, as I understood in writing it, that the press had no right of access superior to that of the general public." This did not bode well for bringing Stewart into our camp.

In preparing my argument, I got help from *New York Times* columnist Anthony Lewis, who had covered the Court for the *Times* and was teaching a First Amendment course at Harvard Law School, where I was a lecturer at the time. He strongly cautioned me against arguing that the press has rights that the public does not have, but I didn't think I had any alternative. Plainly, the general public can't investigate jails; allowing reporters in was the only way to keep the sheriff—and, more broadly, the government—from concealing conditions and information from the public. Lewis brought his class down to Washington for the argument, and we had a post-argument seminar in one of the Court's ornate conference rooms. Lewis's column that week said: "Any editor or reporter who thinks the press is a beloved institution should have been in the Supreme Court chamber the other day. A press claim being argued under the First Amendment drew from the bench extraordinarily open expressions of scorn and hostility." I told the class I felt as though I had been standing before the Court in my pajamas.

Chief Justice Burger interrupted the first sentence out of my mouth. As Lewis reported, hostile questions were accompanied by critical observations: "Members of the Court were especially skeptical of the idea that the press should have greater rights of access . . . than the general public. Justice Byron R. White referred half a dozen times, in sarcastic tones, to 'special privileges' for the press." Justice Rehnquist raised the specter of opening the floodgates to federal constitutional claims every time a government official said no to the press. I tried to calm that concern by referring to Dick Hongisto's testimony that other jails were completely open and that Sheriff Houchins's no-press policy was not justified. That contention provoked Chief Justice Burger to jump in: "Let's say the president wants to have cabinet meetings open to the media, with television and so on. Does that mean that the courts have to open their conferences because someone else does it?" I said it did not, adding: "The only feasible way the public at large will know what's going on in this jail is if reporters are allowed in. A handful of people can go on the tours. But reporters, acting as agents for the public at large— the eyes and ears of the public at large—can go in and without any disruption to jail routine—because it's done in all the other prisons and jails in the area—can meet this public need without interfering with any purpose, valid purpose, of the sheriff."

So far, I had not heard from Justice Stewart. Presently he ventured that perhaps "equal" access could be "provided in a different kind of way," recognizing the special needs of the press. This sounded hopeful. But then he continued: "Well, how far does your argument go? There are many areas wouldn't you agree to which the public does not, in fact, have access, let's say to the Oval Office in the White House . . . [and] to that extent, the public doesn't know what goes on there. . . . We're talking not about policy or prudential considerations or wisdom or lack of it. We're talking about what is required by the First and Fourteenth Amendments." When I reminded him that Sheriff Houchins completely excluded both press and public, Stewart's tone turned sharp: "Why does the mere fact that the public does not have access thereby confer a right upon the press to access? That's a brand new doctrine that I've never heard of. [Members of the press are excluded] from many areas of governmental life. They're excluded from the war room over in the CIA" as well as from deliberations of both courts and commissions.

I tried to distinguish those situations by pointing out that the information discussed in the CIA and in judicial deliberations could properly be considered confidential, while "what's going on in this jail is information that has no claim to confidentiality." I also noted that jails are different kinds of governmental institutions, imprisoning citizens "with an opportunity for overreaching the liberties of the people confined and very little opportunity for that to come to public knowledge unless reporters are permitted in."

Stewart was unconvinced: "There may be other reasons that the public is not given access aside from confidentiality: reasons of security, of discipline, of the very fact that a jail is a jail." I said the Sheriff had not claimed any such interest, driving Stewart to dig in his heels: "He doesn't have to. It's you who are attacking what he has done. It's you saying what he has done is unconstitutional, violative of the U.S. Constitution. He doesn't have to justify it. You have to invalidate it."

It wasn't quite over. Justice Rehnquist asked me whether a reporter could get a jail story by visiting a prisoner during the Sunday visiting hour. I said, "Yes, but you could not see the scene. You have no idea what the conditions look like. Should the press take the prisoner's word for what it looks like and what happened without checking it out? I think not. And certainly my client thinks not."

REHNQUIST: Should the press take the president's press secretary's word for what the president's views are without going into the Oval Office and checking him out?

TURNER: Well, that's the way they do business over there.

This bad answer to a sarcastic question reanimated Stewart.

STEWART: You're dealing here with a constitutional issue.

TURNER: The President of the United States cannot be required to meet the press by any constitutional . . .

BURGER: What about a United States senator? There are normally a hundred of them.

TURNER: I don't think any court could order a senator to sit down and meet with the press.

BURGER: Four hundred thirty-five members of the House?

TURNER: We're not saying that the sheriff has to come out and meet the press or open his files or tell us when anything happened. He just can't shut the door to us on the ground that all that's required is equality even if that equality is zero.

■   ■   ■

On June 26, 1978, the Court handed down its decision. The Court split 3–3–1. Chief Justice Burger wrote an opinion for himself, Rehnquist, and White in which he resoundingly resolved both of the ambiguities left by Stewart's *Pell* decision: "Neither the First Amendment nor the Fourteenth Amendment mandates a right of access to government information or sources of information within the government's control. . . . The media have no special right of access to the Alameda County Jail different from or greater than that accorded the public generally." In other words, *no one* has a First Amendment right of access not only to a jail but to any "government information," and the press has no greater access than the public.

Justice Stevens dissented, in an opinion joined by Justices Brennan and Powell. He reasoned: "Without some protection for the acquisition of information about the operation of public institutions such as prisons by the public at large, the process of self-governance contemplated by the framers would be stripped of its substance. . . . Information gathering is entitled to some measure of constitutional protection." He said that it was important to allow "a democratic community access to knowledge about how its servants were treating some of its members who have been committed to their custody," and he concluded that "an official prison policy of concealing such knowledge from the public by arbitrarily cutting off the flow of information at its source abridges the freedom of speech and of the press."

Justice Stewart was stuck in the middle. He concurred in the judgment that the injunction against the sheriff was unwarranted but thought KQED was entitled to some relief. Unfortunately, he agreed with the Chief Justice that the First Amendment does not guarantee either the public or the press access to government information, and does not give the press any superior right. "The Constitution does no more than assure the public and press equal access once government has opened its doors." However, he said, "The concept of equal access must be accorded more flexibility in order to accommodate the practical distinctions between the press and the general public." He went on to refer to the special status of the press recognized in his "Or of the Press" speech, noted that to do its constitutionally recognized job the press had special needs, and concluded that "terms of access that are reasonably imposed on individual members of the public may, if they impede *effective* reporting without sufficient justification, be unreasonable as applied to journalists." In other words, reporters *are* entitled to greater rights than members of the public. Specifically, Stewart said, reporters should be allowed in the jail when newsworthy events occurred (not just on scheduled tours), and they should be able to use cameras and recording equipment. But since Stewart's theory was that the press was not entitled to access to sources of information not available to the public, reporters could be excluded from the maximum-security part of the jail and could be prohibited from interviewing prisoners. Stewart said he would not preclude the possibility of some injunctive relief for KQED along these lines, but it would "depend on the extent of access then permitted the public."

■　　■　　■

The old chestnut about Supreme Court advocacy, attributed to former attorney general and Supreme Court Justice Robert

Jackson, is that every argument in the Court turns out to be three arguments: the one prepared weeks in advance that is carefully outlined, logical, coherent, and complete; the actual one before the Court, during which the advocate stumbles, is interrupted and incoherent, feels frustrated, and never gets to most of the points in the outline; and finally, the one that comes to the lawyer after going to bed that night, the one that takes a Justice's question and brilliantly turns it into a triumph for the client's cause. I must confess that I have never, in the decades since the *KQED* argument, figured out what that third, clinching argument would have been.

■   ■   ■

I did not realize until much later how close we came to establishing a First Amendment right of access to government facilities and information. For his book *Freedom of the Press*, Professor Bernard Schwartz got access to the private papers of retired justices, including their notes of the conference when they voted on the *KQED* case. It turned out that the Court's initial vote on the case was 4–3 in KQED's favor. The writing of the majority opinion was assigned to Justice Stevens, and his draft was very close to the opinion he eventually filed as a dissent. At some point Justice Stewart, who had voted with Stevens's majority, got cold feet and wrote a note to Stevens taking the position expressed in his concurrence, and Stevens lost his majority. The opinion drafted as a dissent by the Chief Justice became the majority opinion. And an important constitutional principle was lost.

■   ■   ■

By the time the case was returned to the court in San Francisco, Sheriff Houchins had come to appreciate the value of the public tours. They were good public relations. He decided to keep them. This position allowed us, relying on Justice Stewart's fence-straddling concurrence, to settle the case basically along the lines Stewart identified. Because the public was allowed to enter the jail, so were reporters. And, to do the "effective" job referred to by Stewart, they could come whenever a news event occurred and bring the tools of their trade; however, access to the maximum-security part of the jail and interviews with prisoners would not be allowed. This relief, contained in a consent order, was better than nothing. But the loss of a great First Amendment principle still hurt.

Oddly, just two years after the *KQED* decision, the Court decided that there was a First Amendment right of access after all. In 1980, the Court decided the first of four cases in which newspapers contended that they had a right of access to criminal trial proceedings. In an opinion by Chief Justice Burger that did not even mention the *KQED* precedent, the Court determined that in light of the long history of openness of criminal trials and the important practical values served by openness, *both* press and public had a constitutional right of access. The decision was greeted with a touch of irony in Justice Stevens's concurring opinion:

> This is a watershed case. . . . Never before has [the Court] squarely held that the acquisition of newsworthy matter is entitled to any constitutional protection whatsoever. . . . It is somewhat ironic that the Court should find more reason to

recognize a right of access today than it did in *Houchins*. For *Houchins* involved the plight of a segment of society least able to protect itself, an attack on a longstanding policy of concealment, and an absence of any legitimate justification for abridging public access to information about how government operates.

The lack of a more general right of access to government facilities and information puts the United States behind many other democracies. Scandinavian countries in particular give prominent place in their constitutions to freedom of information. Sweden's constitution, for example, enshrines what is basically a freedom of information act as an article in its constitution. Under the Supreme Court's interpretation of *our* constitution, however, government transparency is merely a matter of grace. Officials need not answer questions from citizens or reporters, or allow anyone in the door to look around. Even the right to see documents under the Freedom of Information Act is riddled with exceptions. This situation allows for the kind of excessive secrecy that characterized the administration of George W. Bush and Dick Cheney. For example, shortly after 9/11 hundreds of immigrants, mostly Muslim, were rounded up and threatened with deportation. The administration closed deportation hearings to both press and public, and the immigration court dockets were sealed so that no one could even know if a hearing was scheduled. This regime of secrecy prompted a federal judge to remark: "Democracy dies behind closed doors."

■   ■   ■

Dick Hongisto did not end his career as sheriff. He went on to become the chief of police in Cleveland, under progressive mayor Dennis Kucinich. They did not get along, and Hongisto lasted only three months. He then was chosen by the governor of New York to run the state prisons, but the legislature refused to confirm the appointment. Returning to San Francisco, Hongisto was elected to the city's board of supervisors. In 1992, Mayor Frank Jordan named him Chief of Police.

Hongisto could not have been thinking about lofty First Amendment principles when he picked up the telephone on May 7, 1992, and called Sgt. Gary Delagnes. The week before, after the Rodney King police brutality verdict in Los Angeles, widespread, noisy, and volatile demonstrations broke out in San Francisco. Somewhat uncharacteristically, Hongisto forcefully acted to contain and suppress them. He had the police cordon off an entire neighborhood in the Mission district, and hundreds of people, demonstrators and bystanders, were caught in the net and arrested. Instead of merely citing and releasing those arrested, as would customarily be done, Hongisto arranged for hundreds of them to be taken by bus not to a San Francisco jail but, ironically, to the Alameda County jail at Santa Rita (by then, a new jail, but still not a nice place). They were held in custody for up to 30 hours, preventing them from returning to San Francisco and rejoining the demonstrations.

Hongisto's actions provided the cover story for the May 7, 1992, issue of the *San Francisco Bay Times*, a gay and lesbian weekly newspaper. On the cover was a photograph of Hongisto with a silly grin on his face pasted over the body of someone dressed as a police officer holding a giant baton emerging from his groin as though masturbating. The headline screamed "Dick's Cool New Tool: Martial Law." The article in the paper was highly critical of Hongisto's aggressive police actions. It said that "ex-liberal police chief Hongisto declared martial law," and that his policies represented not only "wholesale suspension of the First Amendment, but also a total abrogation of much of the Constitution." Hongisto had always been supportive of the gay community, and the *Bay Times* cover story must have hurt.

At a police commission meeting the night before, Sergeant Delagnes appeared and in Hongisto's presence vigorously defended Hongisto's actions. When Hongisto called Delagnes the next evening with a copy of the *Bay Times* in his hand, he knew that at the time Delagnes was assigned to the vice squad, worked in plainclothes, drove an unmarked police vehicle, and was on duty until 3:00 a.m. He knew that the *Bay Times* was a free newspaper, distributed in news racks in the Castro neighborhood and elsewhere in the city. He asked Delagnes if he thought they could get "these things out of the racks" and said he would "like to see as many of these off the street as [he could]." Hongisto told Delagnes that he was "very offended" by the cover, that it "bordered on pornography," and the depiction was "somehow beyond the First Amendment."

Since Delagnes was not familiar with the *Bay Times*, Hongisto told him he would leave a copy of the paper on the windshield of his official car while he was attending a meeting. Delagnes fetched the paper, and as he and a fellow officer drove around they read aloud from the critical Hongisto article. While still on duty, Delagnes went to a transvestite bar, asked the owner if he had any copies of the paper, and took the entire bundle from him. Then he drove through the Castro district and observed the location of *Bay Times* news racks.

Near the end of his shift that night and still on duty, Delagnes recruited two other officers and they went out in the dead of night and emptied as many *Bay Times* news racks as they could find, loading the newspapers into the trunk of the police car. One of them pretended to be filling the racks so as to avoid suspicion. Delagnes later testified that he took the papers because he was "repulsed" by the cover: "I thought it was just vile." He was especially concerned because the cover could be seen through the window in the news racks and one of them was "right around the corner from a Catholic church." He added, "The First Amendment is fine and dandy but you know, you got all these kids walking by and they're looking at this stuff and this stuff is really trash." He wanted to get as many papers as he could so they would not be "exposed to the public." The officers confiscated about 3,000 copies and took them to one officer's garage, where they left them. Delagnes and another officer left for Lake Tahoe for the weekend.

The plot unraveled the next Monday when Delagnes told his supervisor what the officers had done. The supervisor, Art Gerrans, called Delagnes back to get the details and secretly tape-recorded the conversation in which Delagnes richly incriminated himself. The matter quickly escalated to the mayor's office. A speedy police commission investigation resulted in Hongisto being fired after only six weeks as chief.

■   ■   ■

When the newspapers disappeared from the racks, and before anyone knew who took them, Kim Corsaro, the editor and publisher of the *Bay Times*, was naturally upset. The newspapers had been stolen from the heart of her distribution area. There was "no visible sign of the paper in the Castro." She hired a private investigator to find out who was stealing the newspapers and a security service to protect company property and personnel, and she tried to refill the emptied racks. She was also distressed when she learned the next week that it was the police who, instead of protecting her business against thieves, were themselves the thieves. She determined to sue Hongisto, the officers, and the city for violating her constitutional rights. I agreed to represent her and the newspaper company. We sued in federal court.

Having fired Hongisto, the City of San Francisco tried to disown him and refused to represent him, claiming that he had not been acting within the scope of his employment. City government officials also contended that the city was not liable to the *Bay Times* as Hongisto's employer, because he was not a "policymaker" for the city. The city's defense lawyers proceeded to subject Corsaro and the *Bay Times* to scorched earth litigation tactics: 115 written interrogatories, 131 document requests, several depositions, 2 separate motions to dismiss, 4 separate motions for summary judgment, and a motion to compel Corsaro to testify about prepublication internal editorial discussions about the cover of the seized newspaper.

When I took Hongisto's deposition before trial, I encountered a different Richard Hongisto than the effusive, forthright witness I had questioned in the *KQED* case. He was tight-lipped, defensive, and suffered convenient memory lapses on key points. He gave rote "I don't recall" answers to the most basic questions. For example, he did not "recall" how he happened to get the copy of the newspaper with his picture on the cover, when he received it, what his first reaction was, whom he talked with on the telephone immediately before and after his call to Delagnes, what he did that evening, what he talked about with the mayor who called and told him the papers had been stolen, and whether he told the officers they should not admit their guilt after they were caught. These lapses would not seem credible to the jury.

The entire shenanigan was so outlandish that there were no First Amendment subtleties. Clearly, government officers were not allowed to confiscate newspapers because they disapproved of the content. Constitutionally, the *Bay Times* depiction of Hongisto was no different from political cartoons that are offensive to their targets but indisputably protected by the First Amendment. And seizing the newspaper was the crudest kind of "prior restraint," a classic violation of the First Amendment. Despite the relative simplicity of the constitutional issues, the defendants conceded nothing.

When the case finally got to trial, even Hongisto's lawyer admitted to the jury in his opening statement that Hongisto thought it was "unfair" for him to be targeted and that he was "hurt" and "embarrassed" by the newspaper's "political lampoon." Hongisto and the officers did contend that because the papers were free, taking them did not violate anyone's rights. But the Supreme Court had made it clear ever since the *Lovell* case in 1938 (establishing the right of a Jehovah's Witness to distribute literature) that First Amendment protection does not depend on whether a publication is sold rather than given away. If it were otherwise, police could confiscate a pamphleteer's political or religious handouts because they are given away on a street corner; or if the government disapproved of a radio or television broadcast, it could jam the frequency because the programming is provided free to listeners and viewers.

Hongisto and the officers tried to convince the jury with a

new defense: that Hongisto wanted the papers collected and then "distributed" to the police rank and file so they could see what he was up against in those trying times. This was of course a pretext. Copies of the paper could legitimately have been brought to the attention of police officers in many obvious ways, and no one suggested any intent to distribute them to the force until after the thieves were caught. When Delagnes told his supervisor what the officers had done, he was caught on tape crowing that he was ready to call Hongisto and announce "Mission accomplished!" even though not a single newspaper had been "distributed" to any police officer. He reported that Hongisto had asked him to "get these things out of the racks," and Delagnes proudly said they "cleaned them out," then laughed heartily.

The jury rejected the police story, returned a verdict in favor of Corsaro and the *Bay Times*, and awarded $35,600 in damages. The city had to indemnify the officers and Hongisto because they were acting within the scope of their employment. No one got rich. But important First Amendment principles were vindicated. It was not Dick Hongisto's finest hour. He fell victim to the not uncommon phenomenon of losing your commitment to the freedoms of speech and press when you are the target.

CLARENCE BRANDENBURG

"Personally, I believe the nigger should be returned to Africa, the Jew returned to Israel," Clarence Brandenburg said. The film showed twelve hooded figures, some of whom carried firearms. They gathered around a large wooden cross, which they burned. The members of the group could be heard saying, "This is what we are going to do to the niggers," "Save America," "Bury the niggers," "Freedom for the whites."

In the late 1960s, Brandenburg was a Ku Klux Klan leader in Cincinnati. He had telephoned a local television station and invited a reporter to come to a Klan rally at a farm in Hamilton County. The reporter, accompanied by a cameraperson, attended the rally and filmed it. During the rally Brandenburg made a speech, in which he said, "We're not a revengent [sic] organization, but if our president, our congress, our Supreme Court continues to suppress the white, Caucasian race, it's possible that there might have to be some revengeance [sic] taken."

Brandenburg was prosecuted under an Ohio criminal syndicalism law of the same vintage as the "red flag" law used to prosecute Yetta Stromberg in California, one of the batch of similar World War I–era laws passed by states out of fear of Bolshevism. The Ohio law made it a felony to "advocate . . . the duty, necessity, or propriety of crime, sabotage, violence, or unlawful methods of terrorism as a means of accomplishing industrial or political reform." Brandenburg was convicted, fined, and sentenced to one to ten years in prison.

■ ■ ■

The clear-and-present-danger test invented by Justice Oliver Wendell Holmes in the *Schenck* case sounded as though it would substantially protect subversive or unpopular speech. It seemed like a real limitation on the power of government to restrict speech and punish dissidents and eccentrics. Unfortunately, as the Court *applied* the test, giving the government the benefit of the doubt in virtually every case, the protection was illusory. As noted in Chapter 2, the Court affirmed the convictions of all the dissidents, anti-war protesters (with the exception of the Jehovah's Witnesses), and Communists from World War I into the Cold War era, finding that their subversive advocacy did indeed create a clear and present danger that the system might be overthrown. The test was toothless.

Clarence Brandenburg's case arrived in the Supreme Court in 1969, in the waning years of the Warren Court. Having decided many cases vindicating the right of civil rights demonstrators to protest racial injustice, would the justices adhere to the clear-and-present-danger test and breathe life into it, or would they abandon it? That the Court came up with a new formulation for dealing with subversive speech at the behest of a Ku Klux Klansman is perhaps odd.

Ironically, Brandenburg's case was argued by a Jew, Allen

Brown, who was counsel for the ACLU in Cincinnati. Helping Brown on the case from the national ACLU was Eleanor Holmes Norton, an African American. (Norton has been the congressperson from the District of Columbia for many years.) At about the same time, Brown was representing a Black Panther as well as the Klansman. Brandenburg, the racist and anti-Semite, did not want a Jew as his lawyer; but he was well represented.

The Court struck down the Ohio law. It acknowledged that it had upheld the very similar California Criminal Syndicalism Act in *Whitney v. California* in 1927, despite the famous and eloquent opinion of Justice Louis Brandeis. But in *Brandenburg* the Court said *Whitney* had been "thoroughly discredited" by later decisions citing, oddly, *Dennis,* the Communist case from the McCarthy era. *Dennis,* of course, had affirmed the convictions of Communist party leaders on the theory that they had conspired to "advocate" overthrow of the government. In the *Dennis* decision, the Court acknowledged the persuasive effect of Holmes's and Brandeis's dissents in the World War I–era cases but did not say that it considered *Whitney* no longer good law. In *Brandenburg,* without mentioning the clear-and-present-danger test, which *had* been applied in the Communist case, the Court announced a new operative principle: "The constitutional guarantees of free speech and free press do not permit a State to forbid or proscribe advocacy of the use of force or of law violation except where such advocacy is directed to inciting or producing imminent lawless action and is likely to incite or produce such action." It added that "mere abstract teaching . . . of the moral propriety or even moral necessity for a resort to force and violence is not the same as preparing a group for violent action and steeling it to such action." Because the Ohio law purported to punish "mere advocacy," it violated the First Amendment. The key distinction is between protected "advocacy" and unprotected "incitement."

■   ■   ■

"Advocacy" of hateful ideas is unlawful in other countries. Speakers are not free to advocate—even in noninflammatory media like books—racial or religious hatred or discrimination, genocide, violence, or violation of law. This restriction is not surprising in countries with painful histories of ethnic and religious cruelty. In several European countries, Holocaust denial is a crime. Even in Scandinavian countries that consistently rank as the freest in the world in speech and press, advocating racial or religious hate is illegal. In Sweden, for example, the Freedom of the Press Act makes it an offense to express "contempt for a population group with allusion to its race, skin colour, national or ethnic origin, or religious faith."

The American constitutional tolerance for advocacy of extremely bad ideas may be unique in the world. The protection for such advocacy, established by Clarence Brandenburg's case, is one of three free-speech features that distinguish the United States from other countries. The others are near-complete freedoms from "prior restraints" and from punishment for defaming public officials. Under the *Pentagon Papers* case, government is not allowed to impose prior restraints—advance censorship—on speech unless it can prove that the speech will in fact cause direct, immediate, and irreparable harm to the national security or some other vital national interest. Under *New York Times v. Sullivan*, we all have a right to criticize government, and public officials and public figures can't sue for libel without proving basically that a defamatory statement is a deliberate lie. These three pillars of free speech—*Pentagon Papers, Sullivan,* and *Brandenburg*—set us apart from the speech protections of other countries. *Brandenburg* is the weakest pillar.

■ ■ ■

The *Brandenburg* rule's shakiness is due both to its origin and to fears generated by international terrorism and extremism at home. The decision itself was a brief unsigned *per curiam* (by the Court) opinion, not usually a sign of a major landmark. The opinion was disingenuous in saying that *Whitney* had been discredited by *Dennis.* The Court also engaged in historical revisionism when it asserted that the convictions in *Dennis* had been upheld only because the repressive Smith Act used to prosecute the Communists "embodied" the very advocacy-incitement principle announced in *Brandenburg;* that was not a fair reading of *Dennis.* Finally, the opinion did not actually say that the Court was abandoning the clear-and-present-danger test and replacing it with the new formulation. This can only be deduced from the concurring opinions of Justices Hugo Black and William Douglas, both First Amendment absolutists. Black flatly said that the clear-and-present-danger test "should have no place in the interpretation of the First Amendment." Douglas elaborated on the history of the test, pointing out how easily it had been "manipulated" to suppress anti-war speech and how in *Dennis* the Court had "distort[ed] the . . . test beyond recognition." Douglas also stated: "The test was so twisted and perverted in *Dennis* as to make the trial of those teachers of Marxism an all-out political trial which was part

and parcel of the cold war that has eroded substantial parts of
the First Amendment." Plainly, Black and Douglas thought the
Court had finally interred the clear-and-present-danger test,
but the Court never squarely said so.

The Court has not retreated from *Brandenburg*. It continues
to rely on it as binding precedent (as Justice Kennedy did in the
child pornography case discussed in Chapter 8) for the point
that government can't outlaw planting bad ideas (like having
sex with children). But some fear that in the perilous atmosphere of the 21st century, infested with both fiery rhetoric
and deadly violence, our security is not adequately safeguarded
under the *Brandenburg* rule. For example, in his book *Freedom
for the Thought That We Hate*, Anthony Lewis expresses particular concern about jihadist terrorist acts that have followed
exhortations in some mosques to attack Western soldiers,
police, and government officials. He points to the 2005 Lon-
don subway killings of 52 people by suicide bombers and to a
militant's statement that the bombings were "praiseworthy."
He also notes that radio broadcasts in Rwanda urged Hutus to
kill Tutsis, and massacres followed. Lewis would not protect
speech that calls for the murder of police and others.

Lewis acknowledges Justice Brandeis's classic statement of
the reasons why we should allow expression of even the most
dangerous ideas. In *Whitney v. California*, Brandeis said:

> [The framers who] won our independence [valued] . . . liberty
> both as an end and as a means. They believed . . . courage to be
> the secret of liberty. They believed that freedom to think as you
> will and to speak as you think are means indispensable to the
> discovery and spread of political truth . . . [and that with free
> speech and assembly] discussion affords ordinarily adequate

protection against the dissemination of noxious doctrine. . . . [They knew] that it is hazardous to discourage thought, hope, and imagination; that fear breeds repression; that repression breeds hate; that hate menaces stable government; that the path of safety lies in the opportunity to discuss freely supposed grievances and proposed remedies; and that the fitting remedy for evil counsels is good ones.

If there is time to expose through discussion the falsity or dangers of noxious speech and avert the evil by educating the people, Brandeis stated: "The remedy to be applied is more speech, not enforced silence."

Lewis seems pessimistic about the prospects of developing good counsels to combat evil ones. He particularly objects to the "imminence" requirement of the *Brandenburg* rule. He says, "I think we should be able to punish speech that urges terrorist violence to an audience some of whose members are ready to act on the urging. That is imminence enough."

I suspect that his concern is not so much about a single incendiary speech as about years of continuous harangues and indoctrination into a culture in which terrorism seems necessary, even religiously required. It may include madrassas and weapons training in Afghanistan or Pakistan, not just attendance at a mosque with a militant cleric. It includes the unshakeable conviction that America has declared war on Islam and conspires with Israel to repress Muslims. The audience is "ready to act" because its members have been primed over months, years, or a lifetime of similar teachings.

I share Lewis's anxiety about terrorism and the susceptibility of some to be galvanized to violence, even suicidal violence, by inflammatory rhetoric. But I am not convinced that

Brandenburg is too lenient a standard. Nor do I think a law can be drafted to silence truly dangerous extremist speech without suppressing a wide range of dissident speech. Brandeis himself, in *Whitney,* said that to justify suppression of speech, "There must be reasonable ground to believe that the danger apprehended is *imminent*" (my italics). He repeated that the evil must be "so imminent that it may befall before there is opportunity for full discussion. . . . Fear of serious injury alone cannot justify suppression of free speech and assembly." In other words, the gravity of the feared harm alone cannot justify suppressing speech; the harm must be imminent. That means no time remains to avert the harm either by preparing to defend against it, by foiling the plot, or by countering the "evil counsels" with "good ones." Rather than attack any particular sermon, we ought to deal with the reasons these impressionable (or hopeless) young people are in a position where they are "ready to act."

This issue is not easy. Consider some hypothetical examples:

- If an anti-abortion preacher calls abortion doctors "baby killers" and urges his congregation in a sermon to "treat them like the murderers they are," and a parishioner two weeks later ambushes and kills a doctor, should the preacher be criminally prosecuted?

- If a conservative radio talk show host calls the president a "socialist" who is "destroying America" and urges listeners to take their guns to the arena where the president is speaking the next day, and a listener gets into the venue and shoots the president, should the host be criminally prosecuted?

- If a Web site posts information on how to make a car bomb, and a site visitor follows the instructions and blows up the police chief's car, should the Web site operator be punished? (Can posting information on a Web site be considered "incitement"?)

I think the answer to each of these questions, under *Brandenburg*, must be *no*. Either no one advocated law violation, or harm is not imminent, or the kind of harm is not reasonably foreseeable, or the speech is not likely to cause a member of the audience to act on the urgings. If you are dissatisfied with that answer, and think that *Brandenburg* puts us at unacceptable risk, I invite you to try your hand at drafting a law that is specific enough to give fair notice to would-be speakers that they risk prosecution and that does not criminalize constitutionally protected speech. What, exactly, would it say? How would it avoid outlawing intemperate religious or political speech? How would it deal with uncertainty whether a deranged listener will be inspired to action? Must the speaker *intend* that violence result? If the harm could have been avoided by alert law enforcement, does that get the speaker off the hook? Is there any reason to believe that the threat of legal punishment would actually deter extremist speech, especially speech by those willing to become martyrs? News broadcasts showing graphic pictures of the Abu Ghraib torture or of women and children killed in their village by a drone bombing seem at least as incendiary as a jihadist speech in a mosque. Should they be outlawed?

I don't think the rule in Clarence Brandenburg's case can be improved on in a way that both makes us safer and still allows militant, disturbing, but protected dissident speech. Aiding and abetting a crime is already illegal, as are *attempting* to commit a crime and initiating or participating in a *conspiracy* to commit a crime. We are dealing here with speech that is still another step removed from a crime—advocacy of committing a crime. If advocacy is itself punishable, whether the criminal behavior urged by the speaker actually occurs does not matter. The speaker can be arrested and charged at once. That is, if the speaker tells his audience members to go out and murder the first police officer they see, the speaker's crime is complete, and he goes to prison even though no one has acted on his urgings. Perhaps the inflammatory rhetoric would not have been persuasive; perhaps no one would have been incited to action; perhaps law enforcement was prepared to intervene and thwart the crime. We would never know.

Exactly 50 years separated *Schenck* from *Brandenburg*. Clarence Brandenburg's case effectively overruled *Schenck, Debs, Whitney,* and the other World War I–era cases, as well as *Dennis* in the Cold War. The case was an unqualified triumph for free speech. The speech found criminal in all those earlier cases was innocuous and posed no real danger either to the Republic or to individual lives. It was seen as unpatriotic, but it is unthinkable today that advocacy of socialism, pacifism, or Communism should have resulted in prison sentences. The rule in Clarence Brandenburg's case—that subversive "incitement" can be punished only if it expressly advocates law violation, calls for imminent law violation, and the violation is likely to occur—is worth keeping. It took us from very little meaningful protection for dissident speech to a level of freedom that is unusual if not unique in the world. That freedom is of course risky, but I think suppression is riskier.

■   ,   ■   ■

In 1955, in the midst of the Cold War, Professor Alexander Meiklejohn, a First Amendment scholar, testified before the Senate Judiciary Subcommittee on the Constitution. He explained that under our Constitution, the people of the United States govern themselves:

> It is they—and no one else—who must pass judgment on public policies. And that means that in our popular discussions, unwise ideas must have a hearing as well as wise ones, dangerous ideas as well as safe, un-American as well as American. . . . The dangers to our safety arising from political suppression are always greater than the dangers to that safety arising from political freedom. Suppression is always foolish. Freedom is always wise. That is the faith, the experimental faith, by which we Americans have undertaken to live.

Meiklejohn was specifically critical of the clear-and-present-danger test, which he said, "has failed to work," "has no dependable meaning," and does not "protect our political freedom." Foreshadowing the Court's decision in *Brandenburg*, Meiklejohn focused on the distinction between advocacy and incitement: "To advocacy, the [First] amendment guarantees freedom, no matter what may be advocated. To incitement, on the other hand, the amendment guarantees nothing whatever." Meiklejohn quoted Brandeis in *Whitney*, whose analysis is the basis of *Brandenburg*: "Advocacy of law-breaking . . . however reprehensible morally, is not a justification for denying free speech where the advocacy falls short of incitement and there is nothing to indicate that the advocacy would be immediately acted on." Meiklejohn concluded by saying, "No belief or advocacy may be denied freedom if, in the same situation, opposing beliefs or advocacies are granted that freedom. If then, on any occasion in the United States, it is allowable to say that the Constitution is a good document, it is equally allowable, in that situation, to say that the Constitution is a bad document. . . . To be afraid of any idea is to be unfit for self-government."

Meiklejohn was courageous to speak up in the mid-50s in defense of the right of Communists to advocate forcible overthrow of the government; doctrinaire Communists would never grant the same freedom to dissenters in Communist countries. That kind of courage is what makes for a First Amendment hero. Clarence Brandenburg probably would not have agreed with Meiklejohn, but his case established a vital First Amendment principle. The principle is fragile, and needs our defending whether we are worried about Communism, racial desegregation, or terrorism.

▪ 8 ▪

LARRY FLYNT

Larry Flynt is no James Madison.

A typical issue of *Hustler* magazine contains well over 100 of what Flynt calls "pink shots," close-up pictures of models' vaginas, sometimes pried open with fingers. That does not make Flynt a First Amendment hero.

Flynt has been prosecuted in various states for publishing "obscene" material. But he has avoided being sent to prison, as the convictions have been overturned on appeal. That does not make him a First Amendment hero.

Every month, *Hustler* publishes an "Asshole of the Month" column, crudely excoriating a politician or other public figure. Several of Flynt's targets have sued him for libel and other wrongs. He has won every suit. That does not make him a First Amendment hero.

On one of his trips to the Supreme Court, when he thought the argument his lawyer made had gone badly, he shouted at the justices: "You're nothing but eight assholes and a token cunt!" Chief Justice Burger ordered him arrested. He has been held in contempt of court on several other occasions, once for wearing an American flag diaper to court. None of this makes him a First Amendment hero.

During the 2008 presidential campaign, Flynt produced a pornographic video called "Who's Nailin' Paylin," featuring an "actress" resembling Republican vice presidential candidate Sarah Palin. The minimal dialogue, interspersed with sex acts, might generously be considered political satire. (Most of the dialogue is "Oh, yes!" and moans.) The "candidate" does say it's "time to drill, baby, drill," and asks, "What are you waiting for, congressional approval?" The "plot" includes a Bill O'Reilly look-alike presiding over "The Orally Factor" as well as a mènage-a-trois with "Hillary" and "Condi" actresses. The video ends with the candidate's announcement: "I'm Serra Paylin, and I approved this message."

Several Web sites put the first minute of the "Paylin" video online for free. When the Huffington Post tried to post more, it was prevented from doing so by Flynt's copyright claim. That definitely does not make Flynt a First Amendment hero. If you're making a political statement, you want as many people as possible to see it; you do not hide behind intellectual property claims. Flynt made half a million dollars on this opportunistic quickie.

In a way, Flynt's life has been *defined* by the First Amendment. He has been prosecuted and sued for the speech he has published, has exposed politicians' hypocrisy in the best First Amendment tradition, has criticized courts and mainstream media for not doing their job, and may be the only person who has literally "taken a bullet" for the First Amendment: He was shot in an assassination attempt during an obscenity trial, and his legs remain paralyzed. But much of his speech has been self-promoting, and virtually all of it has been profit-driven. He has amassed a fortune and lives the Beverly Hills life of the corporate CEO he is. Few would claim that the world's leading pornographer should be considered an unalloyed real world hero. He remains a subject worth considering.

■   ■   ■

Understanding how Flynt has mostly avoided jail and ruinous civil liability requires some background on sexual speech and the First Amendment. "Pornography" is not a legal term. Except for *child* pornography, discussed below, labeling material "pornographic" has no legal consequences. The major legal restriction on sexual speech traditionally has been "obscenity."

The Supreme Court finally settled on a definition of obscenity about the time Flynt began publishing *Hustler*. That seems to be coincidental. The Court had long struggled with identifying precisely what kind of sexual speech, both words and images, could be banned. The assumption had always been that obscenity could be prohibited. It was viewed as a category of speech that is outside First Amendment protection, not because it in fact causes harm but because it is deemed offensive to a civilized society. But the Court, in case after case in the 1950s and 1960s, found grave difficulty in separating in a principled way sexual content that might have some value to society from hard-core sleaze. The Court found it necessary to rescue literature like *Fanny Hill* and the movie of *Lady Chatterley's Lover* from prosecution as obscene. The Court tentatively tried various formulations of the standards for deciding what was or was not obscene but had not come up with a standard that drew the elusive principled line. Justice Potter Stewart famously lamented that arriving at a meaningful definition of hard-core obscenity may not be possible, but he asserted, "I know it when I see it."

In 1973, the Court decided *Miller v. California*. The Court laid down a three-part test for judging whether material is obscene. First, the material, "taken as a whole," must appeal to the "prurient" interest. Second, its depictions of sexual acts must be "patently offensive" as judged by contemporary community standards. Third, the material must lack "serious literary, artistic, political, or scientific value." The *Miller* test was meant to apply to material of all kinds: books, magazines, live performances, movies, and now videos and online communications. The Court has not altered the test in the intervening decades.

The test is not very satisfactory. It cannot be consistently applied. It contains so many subjective elements that it allows juries to punish speech and speakers that they dislike. Professor Kathleen Sullivan has paraphrased the first two parts of the test as material that "turns you on" and material that "grosses you out." She calls these parts "incoherent," requiring the audience to be turned on and grossed out at the same time. Even Justice Antonin Scalia has called for "reexamination" of the test, since whether material has literary or artistic value is a matter of taste, and *"de gustibus non est disputandum."* The test's reliance on "community standards" for judging offensiveness makes no sense as applied to Internet communication, which is available everywhere. Using local standards could subject online material to the standards of the most conservative, least tolerant community. The test is insufficiently protective of speech that may well have some societal value. Fortunately, there are not huge numbers of either federal or state prosecutions. Most of them involve the producers and sellers of raunchy, sometimes violent DVDs.

Instead of emphasizing the pursuit of obscenity prosecutions, in recent years the government has concentrated more on attempts to protect children from exposure to sexual speech and from abuse in the production of sexual material. The Federal Communications Commission (FCC) attempts to police "indecency" on the airwaves, and the Justice Department prosecutes anyone it can catch who possesses or distributes "child pornography."

The FCC has long been empowered by Congress to regulate "indecent" material on radio and television. But it didn't really try to enforce the law until the "family values" forces became a political factor and demanded that the commission prevent broadcasters from airing vulgar language or programs with sexual content at times when children might be in the audience. The commission's constitutional authority to regulate dirty words or pictures was not tested until 1978, when the Supreme Court decided *FCC v. Pacifica Foundation*. One afternoon a Pacifica radio station aired comedian and satirist George Carlin's famous monologue, "Seven Words You Can Never Say on Television." In the recorded live performance Carlin, with wit and erudition, recited and repeated in various contexts the words that he said cannot be uttered on the airwaves: *fuck*, *shit*, *cocksucker*, *motherfucker*, *piss*, *cunt*, and *tits*. He analyzed their derivation and modern colloquial usage. While driving his boy home from school, a man heard the monologue and complained to the FCC. The Commission decided to reprimand the station for broadcasting "indecent" speech during hours when children might be in the audience.

Pacifica challenged the FCC action, contending that the Carlin monologue was not obscene and that the Commission was barred by the First Amendment from punishing mere "indecency" as opposed to "obscenity." Alas, in a dark day for the First Amendment, the Supreme Court upheld the Commission's position. The opinion was written by Justice John Paul Stevens when he was relatively new to the Court. Judging by his subsequently expressed First Amendment views, Stevens seems to have distanced himself from *Pacifica*. (For example, he wrote the decision invalidating the Communications Decency Act and opined in a later case that criminal prosecutions are an "inappropriate means" to regulate even obscenity.) But in 1978, Stevens's opinion unleashed FCC enforcement against indecency. The opinion said that indecent speech "lies at the periphery of First Amendment concerns." It also emphasized that, as established by earlier Court decisions, the broadcasting medium enjoys the least First Amendment protection (as compared, for example, to newspapers). Broadcasting, Stevens said, was "uniquely pervasive" and "uniquely accessible to children." An administrative sanction, as contrasted with a criminal prosecution, was an appropriate way of protecting children from unwanted exposure to indecent material. Justice Stevens concluded: "We simply hold that, when the commission finds that a pig has entered the parlor, the exercise of its regulatory power does not depend on proof that the pig is obscene."

During the administration of President George W. Bush, his FCC commissioners, encouraged and abetted by Congress, picked up *Pacifica* and ran with it. The commission used a regulation that outlawed airing "language or material that depicts or describes, in terms patently offensive as measured by contemporary community standards for the broadcast medium, sexual or excretory activities or organs."

Notice that this definition of *indecency* borrows one-third of the *Miller* definition of *obscenity*: the "patently offensive" (or "grosses you out") part. It ignores the other two parts. Therefore, material can be found "indecent" even though it does not appeal to the prurient interest at all (saying "Shit!" for example), and even though the material may well have significant "literary, artistic, political or scientific value." The fact that material deemed indecent by the commission may, like Carlin's satirical monologue, have political, artistic, or other societal value makes the prohibition extremely problematical for First Amendment purposes.

The commission began to impose substantial fines on broadcasters who aired any of Carlin's dirty words. In 2006, Congress increased tenfold the maximum fines that the commission could impose, to $325,000 per violation. The energized commission also abandoned its previous policy under which sanctions could be imposed only for "repetitive, deliberate" use of indecent words, and began imposing fines for the airing of a single "fleeting expletive." Notoriously, the FCC fined CBS $550,000 for the split-second "wardrobe malfunction" revealing Janet Jackson's breast during the 2004 Super Bowl half-time show. It announced the new "fleeting expletive" policy when Bono said, upon receiving a Golden Globe award, "This is really, really, fucking brilliant." And it called Fox Television on the carpet when it aired Cher's defiant statement at the Billboard Music Awards, confronting those who said she was washed up: "I've also had critics for the last 40 years saying that I was on my way out every year. Right. So fuck 'em." It again issued an order against Fox when Nicole Richie said at the next year's Awards: "Have you ever tried to get cow shit out of a Prada purse? It's not so fucking simple."

On April 28, 2009, the Supreme Court upheld the FCC's "fleeting expletives" policy shift without reaching the question whether it violates the First Amendment. Justice Scalia's opinion squeamishly referred to Cher's "F-word" and Richie's "S-word," and reported that Bono had exclaimed "f***ing brilliant." The Court decided only that the FCC had not acted arbitrarily in suddenly adopting the fleeting expletives policy, postponing the First Amendment issue for another day. Justice Stevens dissented.

One hopes this ridiculous indecency enforcement will fizzle out, or the Court will revisit *Pacifica* and overrule it. The commission does not regulate indecency on cable (because cable is a subscription service that people pay for and does not use the limited broadcast frequencies available on the electromagnetic spectrum, and because the FCC thinks the Court would therefore not allow regulation of indecency on cable). Given the many opportunities for minors to be exposed to sexual material on the Internet, at school, and in life, there is no good reason for the government to be policing dirty words on radio and over-the-air television. We should cleanse the airwaves not of expletives but of censorship.

The government is actively prosecuting child pornography cases. The laws prohibit pictures of minors performing sex acts and the "lewd" exhibition of their genitals. Like the FCC indecency regulation, the laws do not require appeal to the prurient interest, and it doesn't matter if the pictures arguably have artistic or scientific value. The Supreme Court has decided that sexually explicit pictures of real children do not need to be obscene to be illegal. The reason for this strict prohibition is that the *production* of the pornography is essentially child abuse—children are abused in the process of filming the pictures. Consequently, child pornography is legally toxic, even more than obscenity. While both obscenity and child pornography lack any First Amendment protection, a consumer cannot be prosecuted for having obscene material in the privacy of his home, but mere possession of child pornography is a crime.

Some editorial material and ads in *Hustler* magazine use young-looking models with captions saying they are, for example, "barely legal," playing to readers' interest in teenage temptresses. Flynt also publishes, among 25 other adult magazines, one entitled "Barely Legal." But *Hustler* says it keeps records of its models' ages as required by federal law, and it dutifully publishes the required statement that "all nude models are 18 years of age or older." Child pornography seems to be a business for amateurs, not sophisticated publishers. Flynt himself believes child pornography should be banned as violating the rights of people not old enough to consent. But he says that among consenting adults, material involving sexuality should be their own business.

■   ■   ■

Alongside the dozens of pink shots in an issue of *Hustler* is some serious political writing. For example, a typical 2009 issue had full-page columns by Robert Scheer, Nat Hentoff, and Alex Bennett. It also had a vicious cartoon lampooning Rush Limbaugh, another cartoon in which God "tortures" George W. Bush to get the "truth" by urinating on him, and a tame but serious anti-war cartoon. (Flynt says war is what is obscene.) The Asshole-of-the-Month target was Congresswoman Jane Harmon, taken to task in vulgar terms over her attempt to get appointed chair of the House Intelligence Committee. The issue's Publisher's Statement by Flynt was "Is It Socialism?" a simplistic defense of President Obama's health care and other programs. (The Flynt column was on a page facing a very graphic pink shot advertising phone sex.) All the political material was in the first 21 pages of the magazine.

The balance of the magazine consisted overwhelmingly of sexually explicit pictures and pornographic articles, interspersed with extremely blunt advertisements for sex toys and phone sex. Indeed, by far the biggest section of the issue was 28 straight full pages of phone sex ads, all luridly illustrated.

Flynt's autobiography provides clues to his business strategy. According to Flynt, the "text" of adult magazines doesn't "make a damn bit of difference," as lonely men "read them with one hand." Flynt's magazines are more sexually explicit than men's magazines like *Playboy* and *Penthouse*, and he doesn't care if he frightens away advertisers because he charges $11.99 for the magazine. "The vulgar nature of our cartoons and features [is] a matter of editorial policy. We . . . intentionally try to offend people," he admits.

Flynt seems to try to avoid entanglement with the legal system by putting on the cover of each issue, in microscopic type, the following: "WARNING: Material is of an adult nature. This literature is not intended for minors, and under no circumstances are they to view it, possess it, or place orders for merchandise offered herein." The "literature" referred to apparently is not the political material, for there is no reason why minors should be shielded from it. Rather, a cynic might conclude that claiming "literature" status is a transparent attempt to squeeze within the *Miller* obscenity definition's allowance for literary value. In fact, the pages of political material probably insulate *Hustler* from obscenity prosecution because, under *Miller,* the work "taken as a whole" must be considered, and no court could conclude that a *Hustler* issue lacks political value.

■   ■   ■

The inside front cover of the November 1983 issue of *Hustler* featured a full-page parody of an advertisement for Campari liqueur. It was a takeoff on a Campari advertising campaign in which celebrities were interviewed about their "first time." By the end of the interviews it was clear that the celebrities meant the first time they tried Campari, but the ads played on the sexual double entendre. *Hustler's* version had a picture of the Reverend Jerry Falwell and was headlined "Jerry Falwell talks about his first time." Falwell was of course the leader of the Moral Majority, a major figure in the religious right, a frequent critic of pornography, and a frequent target of Larry Flynt's wrath. The fake Campari ad featured an "interview" with Falwell, who said his first time was with his mother in an outhouse. The ad "quoted" Falwell as saying, "I never really expected to make it with Mom, but then after she showed all the other guys in town such a good time, I figured, 'What the hell!'" In the ad Falwell says: "We were drunk off our God-fearing asses. . . . Mom looked better than a Baptist whore with a $100 donation." The parody concluded with Falwell claiming: "I always get sloshed before I go out to the pulpit. You don't think I could lay down all that bullshit sober, do you?" In tiny type at the bottom of the page was the disclaimer: "Ad parody—not to be taken seriously."

The parody was not legally obscene and clearly not child pornography. Nor, not having been broadcast, could it be restricted as indecency. It was a vicious dirty joke, but Falwell took it seriously. He sued Flynt and *Hustler*, seeking $45 million in damages for libel, for using Falwell's picture for commercial purposes, and for intentionally inflicting emotional distress. To win the emotional distress claim, Falwell would have had to prove that Flynt had a blameworthy state of mind in publishing the humiliating ad. Flynt cooperated in supplying that proof, for at his deposition he testified as follows:

FALWELL'S ATTORNEY: Did you want to upset Rev. Falwell?

FLYNT: Yes . . .

FALWELL'S ATTORNEY: Do you recognize that in having published what you did in this ad, you were attempting to convey to the people who read it that Rev. Falwell was just as you characterized him, a liar?

FLYNT: Yeah, he's a liar too.

FALWELL'S ATTORNEY: How about a hypocrite?

FLYNT: Yeah.

FALWELL'S ATTORNEY: That's what you wanted to convey?

FLYNT: Yeah.

FALWELL'S ATTORNEY: Did you appreciate, at the time that you wrote "okay" to approve this publication, that for Rev. Falwell to function in his livelihood, and in his commitment and career, he has to have an integrity that people believe in? Did you not appreciate that?

FLYNT: Yeah.

FALWELL'S ATTORNEY: And wasn't one of your objectives to destroy that integrity, or harm it, if you could?

FLYNT: To assassinate it.

Falwell's commercial-use-of-his-likeness claim was dismissed by the trial judge. In fact, Falwell himself had duplicated the ad thousands of times and included it in a mass mailing fund-raising plea to Moral Majority supporters around the country, apparently to demonstrate to them the depths to which pornographers can sink, and he netted about $800,000. While this might cast doubt on how much emotional distress the ad caused him, the claims of intentional infliction and libel proceeded to trial.

The jury found against Falwell on the libel claim, deciding that no reasonable reader of the magazine would conclude that any of the parody ad's allegations was factual. Since no one could believe it was true that Falwell had sex with his mother in an outhouse, there could be no libel (a false statement of fact). But the jury found that Flynt had intentionally inflicted emotional distress on Falwell. This verdict depended on the jury's finding that Flynt had acted intentionally, that his conduct offended generally accepted standards of decency or morality (or, in shorthand, was "outrageous"), and that his conduct actually caused Falwell severe emotional distress. The jury awarded Falwell $100,000 in compensatory damages and another $100,000 in punitive damages. Flynt took the case to the Supreme Court.

■   ■   ■

The Court handed down its decision on February 24, 1988. Ominously, the opinion was written by Chief Justice William Rehnquist. Always conservative and nearly always unfriendly to civil liberties claims, Rehnquist could not realistically have been expected to say anything to help Flynt's cause. But in virtually the only good First Amendment opinion he wrote in his entire career, Rehnquist led a unanimous court to rule in Flynt's favor. The opinion makes an important contribution to First Amendment freedoms for all of us.

Rehnquist framed the issue: "We must decide whether a public figure may recover damages for emotional harm caused by the publication of an ad parody offensive to him, and doubtless gross and repugnant in the eyes of most." The court acknowledged that the *Hustler* parody was both "patently offensive" and "intended to inflict emotional injury." But then Rehnquist launched into a rhapsodic treatment of First Amendment values, even quoting Justice Oliver Wendell Holmes's "marketplace of ideas" concept from his famous *Abrams* dissent. Rehnquist reminded everyone: "Robust political debate encouraged by the First Amendment is bound to produce speech that is critical [of public figures]." The question was whether the speech lost First Amendment protection because of the speaker's bad motives.

At the argument in the Supreme Court, Rev. Falwell's lawyer, Norman Grutman, began by asserting: "Deliberate, malicious character assassination is not protected by the First Amendment." Rehnquist's opinion confronted this argument by noting, "In the world of debate about public affairs, many things done with motives that are less than admirable are protected by the First Amendment." The debate would be inhibited if the speaker had to run the risk that it might be proved in court that he spoke out of hatred. Rehnquist continued, "Even if he did speak out of hatred, utterances honestly believed contribute to the free interchange of ideas and the ascertainment of truth." So the intent to hurt someone's feelings does not deprive the speaker of First Amendment protection.

Were the Court to hold otherwise, political cartoonists and satirists would be subjected to damages awards, Rehnquist said. A history buff, Rehnquist clearly was influenced by an *amicus curiae* brief filed by the Association of American Editorial Cartoonists. The brief included an appendix with a collection of famous and infamous political cartoons through American history, including Thomas Nast's savage attacks on "Boss" Tweed, depicting Tweed and his cohorts as "vultures, tyrants, bloated opportunists, and boozy degenerates"; David Levine's caricature of Senator Joseph McCarthy on a witch hunt; and Doug Marlette's portrait of Interior Secretary James Watt in his office with a stuffed trophy head of Bambi adorning his wall. "Our political discourse would have been considerably poorer," Rehnquist said, without this kind of "intentionally injurious speech."

Falwell argued, however, that the fake Campari ad was so "outrageous," as the jury found, as to distinguish it from more traditional political cartoons. Rehnquist acknowledged that the ad was "at best a distant cousin of the political cartoons described above, and a rather poor relation at that." He said that if it were possible to lay down a "principled standard" to separate the two, public discourse probably would not suffer harm. "But," he added, "we doubt that there is any such standard, and we are quite sure that the pejorative description 'outrageous' does not supply one." Rehnquist said that outrageousness is inherently subjective and would allow a jury to award damages based on jurors' tastes or views or dislike of the speech or speaker. (The same would seem to be true of the "patently offensive" standard used for obscenity or indecency, but that was not the issue before the Court.) Rehnquist concluded that an outrageousness standard thus ran afoul of the First Amendment principle first espoused in the Jehovah's Witnesses cases that protects speech even though it "may have an adverse emotional impact on the audience." Plucking a First Amendment jewel from the otherwise regrettable opinion in *FCC v. Pacifica*, Rehnquist emphasized: "The fact that society may find speech offensive is not a sufficient reason for suppressing it."

The Court's decision in *Hustler Magazine v. Falwell* is a charter of liberty for political cartooning and satire. It is also, in the world of litigation, an important protection for publishers because, if public figures or officials claim injury from published material, they must confront and clear First Amendment hurdles—regardless of the label a fertile-minded lawyer might put on their suit ("intentional infliction of emotional distress," libel, or something else). Finally, the Court's decision made it resoundingly clear that speech offensive to its target, and even to the public generally, is not without First Amendment protection. In many countries, publishing an insult of a public official or figure would land the publisher in jail. Not here.

■　■　■

Following the decision, Flynt himself became the subject of unflattering editorial cartoons. The *Washington Times* showed an outhouse with a *Hustler* sign and a robed judge calling to the occupant: "Good news, Mr. Flynt . . . You won!" Pat Oliphant for the *Los Angeles Times* syndicate pictured Flynt as a fat, smelly pig in a wheelchair, with a note from the cartoonist stating: "Dear Mr. Flynt, in order to defend their constitutional freedom of expression, satirists are forced, from time to time, into reluctant association with people like you. In celebration of the excellent Supreme Court decision (*Hustler v. Falwell*), I trust you will accept the accompanying depiction of yourself as strictly satirical."

In recent years a provocative sequence of loosely connected cartoons illustrates one of the points of *Hustler v. Falwell*. In September 2005 a small Danish newspaper, *Jyllands-Posten*, published 12 caricatures of the Prophet Muhammad. The most inflammatory one depicted him wearing a turban in the shape of a bomb with a lit fuse. News of the cartoons spread through the Islamic world. More than 100 people were killed in riots triggered by what some Islamic leaders called blasphemy, and a boycott of Danish goods was organized. (Historically, blasphemy and obscenity were related, and both were considered unprotected speech.) President Mahmoud Ahmadinejad of Iran then organized a "Holocaust Cartoon Contest" and invited Muslim cartoonists to submit cartoons ridiculing the Holocaust and the State of Israel. The winner showed Israeli construction equipment in the West Bank walling off a mosque, with a mural of Auschwitz painted on the wall. During the 2008 presidential campaign, the *New Yorker* ran a cover depicting Michelle Obama as a 60s-style Black Panther toting an AK-47, fist-bumping Barack Obama dressed as a Muslim in the Oval Office under a portrait of Osama bin Laden, with an

American flag burning in the fireplace. The cover was apparently meant to satirize not the Obamas but the lunatic fringe who was saying such things about them, but this subtlety was lost on many. The *Los Angeles Daily News* responded with a cartoon satirizing the *New Yorker* one; it showed President Bush in the militant outfit fist-bumping Vice President Cheney dressed as a Muslim under a dark portrait of Richard Nixon, with the Constitution burning in the fireplace. *Vanity Fair* commissioned a cover showing John and Cindy McCain in the Oval Office, the candidate with a walker and Mrs. McCain with a handful of pills, under a portrait of Bush while the Constitution goes up in flames.

All of these caricatures were somewhat mean-spirited. All might be considered "outrageous" by many, and in poor taste. All would upset their targets and cause hurt feelings, as the *Bay Times* Hongisto cover did. And all of them, after *Hustler v. Falwell*, unquestionably are protected by the First Amendment.

■　■　■

Another *Hustler* case may make it harder to accept Larry Flynt as a First Amendment hero, but the court got it right. The August, 1981, issue included an article titled "Orgasm of Death." It discussed the practice of autoerotic asphyxia: masturbation while hanging oneself to cut off temporarily the blood supply to the brain at the moment of orgasm, intensifying the orgasm. The article was part of a series on "Sexplay," describing practices that have "remained hidden for too long behind the doors of fear, ignorance, inexperience, and hypocrisy," presented to increase readers' sexual knowledge, lessen their inhibitions, and make them "much better lovers."

An editor's note at the top of the article said that *"Hustler* emphasizes the often-fatal dangers of the practice of auto-erotic asphyxia and recommends that readers seeking unique forms of sexual release DO NOT ATTEMPT this method." The article began with an arresting description of the tragic results from trying the practice, saying that as many as 1,000 American teenagers die in this manner every year. The two-page article warned readers 10 different times that the practice is dangerous and deadly.

Troy D, a 14 year old in Houston, came into possession of the magazine and read the article. The next morning his best friend found Troy, nude, hanging by his neck in his closet, with a copy of the magazine opened to the "Orgasm of Death" article at his feet. Troy's mother sued *Hustler* for damages for causing Troy's death. The jury awarded damages totaling $182,000, and *Hustler* appealed.

Judge Alvin Rubin of the Fifth Circuit Court of Appeals began his analysis by noting that First Amendment protection is "not based on the naïve belief that speech can do no harm but on the confidence that the benefits society reaps from the free flow and exchange of ideas outweigh the costs society endures by receiving reprehensible or dangerous ideas." Noting that there is "no such thing as a false idea," Rubin said we correct pernicious ideas not by suppressing them but by the competition of other ideas: "We rely on a reverse Gresham's law, trusting good ideas to drive out bad ones and forbidding governmental intervention into the free market of ideas." Against the important social goal of protecting adolescents like Troy, the court must balance not just *Hustler*'s right to speak but also the danger that unclear standards of First Amendment protection may inhibit the expression of ideas by other speakers and "constrict the right of the public to receive those ideas."

Troy's mother's case was based on the theory that the *Hustler* article constituted "incitement" and was therefore in a category of speech that has no First Amendment protection, like libel, obscenity, and "fighting words." As noted in Chapter 7, *Brandenburg v. Ohio* held that "advocacy" of even hateful ideas was constitutionally protected, but speech "directed to inciting or producing imminent lawless action," and likely to produce such action, was not. The Court thus distinguished between protected "advocacy" and unprotected "incitement." (The difference in my mind is between an article articulating the writer's reasons for favoring racial segregation [advocacy, even of bad ideas] and a demonstrator climbing on the barricades with a lighted torch screaming at the unruly mob behind him, "Let's burn it down!" [incitement].)

Judge Rubin decided that the *Hustler* article on autoerotic asphyxia could not be considered incitement: "No fair reading of it can make its content advocacy, let alone incitement to engage in the practice." He doubted that "*written* material might ever be found to create culpable incitement," but was clear that this article, hedged as it was with multiple warnings and blunt advice *not* to try autoerotic asphyxia, was a far cry from incitement.

Judge Edith Jones filed a passionate dissent, contending that the majority had foreclosed the state from tempering "the excesses of the pornography business by imposing civil liability for harms it directly causes." She said the court should protect children against "suicidal pornography," and the court's opinion degraded "the free market of ideas to a level with the black market for heroin." She said, "No federal court has held that death is a legitimate price to pay for freedom of speech."

Jones reasoned that *"Hustler* is not a bona fide competitor in the 'marketplace of ideas.' It is largely pornographic [in that] the principal function of this magazine is to create sexual arousal." Its appeal is "non-cognitive," and "the opposite of the transmission of ideas." Furthermore, Jones said, "A significant portion of its readers are adolescent. *Hustler* knows this. Such readers are particularly vulnerable to thrill-seeking, recklessness, and mimicry." She added that, for them, warnings and saying "No" or "Caution" are "invitations rather than taboos." In other words, *Hustler*, as pornography, should not be protected by the First Amendment against liability for the harm it causes.

Tempting as it is to agree with Jones's rhetorical flourish that the price of free speech should not be death, this is a false choice. To define "pornography" in a way that would not outlaw a significant amount of protected and even valuable speech is impossible. Just try. Once you go beyond the definition of obscenity and make illegal material that may have literary, artistic, or other value, you put a wide range of speech at risk. Moreover, under Judge Jones's approach, speakers could never know when publishing *truthful* information, with or without warnings and disclaimers, might lead some reader to act in a way that harms himself or some other person. Publishers can't be liable to the world at large—to anyone who might pick up the book or magazine, get a bad idea, and act on it, and to others who may be hurt by the reader—for publishing information that turns out to result in harm. We can't shut down *Hustler* without impoverishing the store of information and ideas available to all of us.

■ ■ ■

After the oral argument in the *Falwell* case, Larry Flynt met with a crowd of reporters and onlookers on the steps of the Court building. Asked whether he thought he could win the case, he said, "If the Court will protect a scumbag like me, then it will protect all of you. Because I'm the worst."

· 9 ·

CLINTON FEIN
and the ACLU

Clinton Fein felt betrayed. He thought he had been promised freedom of expression. Instead he got the Communications Decency Act.

Born in South Africa, Fein grew up under Apartheid. As he graduated from the University of Witwatersrand, he was interested in journalism. But the South Africa of the time was not a promising environment for young journalists. Under the repressive censorship regime, one could be imprisoned for quoting Nelson Mandela, who was then in prison for revolutionary activities. Fein emigrated to the United States, studied for citizenship, learned all about the Constitution, and was naturalized in 1994. When he took the oath, he was bemused by the seeming contradiction in having to swear to God to defend a constitution that prohibited any religious coercion. But his primary allegiance, and hope, lay with the First Amendment's free-speech clause. Then Congress enacted, and President Bill Clinton signed, the Communications Decency Act of 1996. As a result, because his speech was online and subject to the Act, Fein would have had freer speech in South Africa, which by that time was post-Apartheid, than he had in the United States. Fein's sense of betrayal propelled him to the federal courthouse.

■ ■ ■

The act, called the CDA, was the most sweeping restriction of the speech of ordinary citizens that Congress had ever attempted. It was more threatening to the average person than the Sedition Act of 1798, in that it was global in its reach and less clear about what was prohibited. It had two main provisions. One made it a federal crime to communicate anything "indecent" online, knowing that the communication was to a minor (17 or under). The term "indecent" was not defined at all. The other made it a crime to "display" on the Internet anything "patently offensive" if it was "available" to a minor (as virtually everything is). Offensiveness would be judged by contemporary "community standards" similar to the way the FCC defined indecency for broadcast purposes. Violation of either provision was punishable by two years in prison and a fine.

The stated purpose of the CDA was to shield children from exposure to indecent online material. Every politician wants to protect America's children from pornography. Few politicians are willing to invoke the First Amendment to defend smut peddlers. The CDA was an act of legislative cowardice. Any modestly intelligent Congressperson had to know that the clumsily drafted CDA was unconstitutional. Passing the law meant dumping responsibility for saying so on the courts.

The CDA was promptly challenged by the ACLU and other organizations. The federal district court in Philadelphia issued a preliminary injunction preventing the government from enforcing the law during the lawsuit. The court thoroughly examined the nature of the Internet and online communications, and found that the CDA would criminalize a vast range of speech that Americans, at least adults, had a right to engage in. For example, if "indecent" means the same thing as it does in the FCC broadcast regulations (Chapter 8), using any of George Carlin's dirty words in an email to a 17-year-old or on any Web site "available" to a minor would be a felony. Posting online the Supreme Court's decision in the *Pacifica* case would be a felony because the Court appended a transcript of the Carlin monologue to it. "Displaying" online great works of art such as Tony Kushner's Pulitzer Prize–winning play *Angels in America*, which has plenty of rough language and sex scenes, would be criminal. So would posting the Attorney General's 1986 Report on Pornography, which described pornographic materials in some detail. Magazines like *Wired* that appeared both in print and online and used some of Carlin's words would be protected on the newsstand but subject to criminal prosecution when editors pressed the button to post an article online. And because offensiveness would be judged by "community" standards, only material bland enough to pass muster in the most conservative, least tolerant community could safely be communicated.

■   ■   ■

At the time the CDA was enacted, self-taught computer whiz Clinton Fein's day job was constructing and maintaining Web sites. But he also had begun publishing edgy, provocative material that attracted the government's attention. He made a CD-ROM of Randy Shilts's book *Conduct Unbecoming: Gays and Lesbians in the U.S. Military*. It included material about a sailor pictured in a Navy recruiting poster who turned out to be gay and was discharged by the Navy. The Navy claimed that Fein could not legally use the picture and said it was protected by trademark law. Fein managed to find help from Michael Traynor, a prominent San Francisco lawyer, who wrote to the Navy that it could not prevent Fein from using the image on trademark or any other legal ground, and the Navy gave up. At the time, Traynor and I were representing *Wired* magazine in various First Amendment–related matters, and we were concerned about the CDA's impact. We met with Fein, who wanted to challenge the CDA in any way he could. So we helped him have his day in court.

Our main attack was on a provision of the CDA different from the ones in the *ACLU* case. It was an update of the old federal "obscene telephone call" statute. As part of the CDA, Congress amended the law to make it a crime, punishable by two years in prison and a fine, to say anything "obscene, lewd, lascivious, filthy, or indecent" using a telecommunications device (defined to include both telephones and computer modems) with intent to "annoy" another person. Fein himself was annoyed, and wanted to annoy the politicians and the prudes who egged them on. So he launched a Web site called annoy.com, which he announced was its own CDA: "Created and Designed to Annoy."

Annoy.com had several innovative features, using cutting-edge technology. One was "heckle," which enabled site visitors to construct and send email messages, anonymously, to various public officials and public figures. It operated like the popular MadLibs game and invited visitors to criticize the recipients in the most vulgar (and hilarious) terms. Most of the messages predictably would "annoy" the recipients. For example, one could compose a letter to speaker of the house Newt Gingrich. It might say "Dear Speaker Gingrich, Your Contract with America is [brilliant/a pile of shit]. It will [save/ruin] America. It will benefit [all Americans/only the rich]. You are truly [a genius/an asshole]."

Another feature was "censure," which allowed visitors to send digital postcards via the Internet. Hallmark greetings these were not. No floral designs or cuddly animals. Some of the cards were sexually explicit and all were provocative. "Gibe" was a message board on which visitors could post messages anonymously. Fein and other writers contributed essays containing language and ideas that might well be considered "indecent" in some communities. The issues they discussed included same-sex marriage, gays in the military, health care, and the environment. Fein was not shy about announcing that the site made it possible for visitors, using "whatever language or imagery seems to them appropriate" to "annoy" public officials and public figures "by getting their attention, upsetting them, and making them understand the depth of displeasure with their acts or political positions." For example, Fein added, "Some of us wish to criticize President Clinton, Speaker Newt Gingrich, Senators Dianne Feinstein, James Exon, and Jesse Helms," and others "because of their role in proposing, enacting, and approving the Communications Decency Act."

The problem with annoy.com was that, if the CDA was constitutional, Fein was subject to criminal prosecution for violating both the statutory prohibition on posting "indecency" and the online communication of "indecent" material "with intent to annoy." So we mounted a two-pronged attack.

First, we filed a brief *amicus curiae* in the Supreme Court in the ACLU's suit. There, we attacked the constitutionality and, indeed, the rationality of the CDA. We made some arguments not made by the ACLU and other parties. We questioned, for example, whether the federal government had the authority under the Constitution to regulate content on the Internet at all and whether the government had a "compelling" interest in meddling in what is first and foremost the domain of parents, not government: what speech their children would have access to. Second, we filed our own suit against attorney general Janet Reno in federal court in San Francisco, seeking to enjoin her from enforcing the "intent to annoy" law. (Reno was my law school classmate; I find it hard to believe that she could endorse the arguments that her underlings made on her behalf to support the CDA.)

Our case was much stronger than the ACLU's because the statute we were challenging had nothing to do with children. The government could not defend it on the ground that it was needed to protect children from indecency. The statute was a flat-out ban on speech that adults have every right to communicate. The fact that a communication was made with intent "to annoy" the recipient could not save the law. As *Hustler v. Falwell* and the Jehovah's Witnesses cases amply demonstrate, government cannot ban speech on the ground that it is offensive, motivated by hatred, or upsetting to the recipient.

The government repeatedly requested more time to respond to our suit and pointed out that the ACLU's case, then pending in the Supreme Court, would likely affect the issues in our case. The government insisted, however, on its right to prosecute Fein for any violations of the CDA provision criminalizing communications with intent to "annoy" that might be committed while the case was delayed. The three-judge court in San Francisco deferred any ruling until *Reno v. ACLU* came down, leaving Fein at risk if he continued to operate annoy .com. He continued.

■   ■   ■

On June 26, 1997, the Supreme Court decided the *ACLU* case. The decision was wonderful, a true landmark of First Amendment freedom. The opinion was written by Justice John Paul Stevens, who thereby redeemed himself from his *Pacifica* blunder discussed in Chapter 8. He now can be considered for candidacy in the pantheon of First Amendment heroes.

Reno v. ACLU was the Court's first Internet case. This was a new medium of communication, and no one could know how the Court might apply First Amendment rules to it. In the past, when confronted with having to decide how the First Amendment applies to a given medium, the Court had sometimes fumbled. For example, when movies were invented and became commercial, the Court in 1915 allowed cities to censor them at will, reasoning that movies were just a business like any other, subject to local regulation, and were not protected by speech or press guarantees. (That ruling was not overruled until 1952.) Also, when the Court had to decide the extent to which cable television could be regulated, the justices were unable to agree on the proper First Amendment analysis.

Stevens got it right in the *ACLU* case. His opinion first laid out in detail how the Internet works and the various ways in which people can communicate on it. Seventy-seven years old at the time, Stevens casually noted that "navigating the Web is relatively straightforward," and then proceeded to explain it in commonsense terms. He had to confront the government's argument that the Internet should be treated like broadcast, subject to government regulation similar to the FCC's regulation of radio and broadcast television. Indeed, the government urged that "the indecency problem" on the Internet was "much more pronounced than it is on broadcast stations." This was because, Attorney General Reno's lieutenants said, the Internet operates "without the intervention of editors, network censors, or market disincentives." In other words, the government argued that because ordinary citizens could communicate with each other directly, not as the passive recipients of programming directed at them by powerful corporations and their commercial sponsors, the government must step in to police "indecent" material. (The perverse result would be that the more democratic the medium—free of corporate censors and commercial "disincentives"—the greater the government's right to regulate the medium.)

Stevens demolished the government's argument, pointing out that the broadcast decisions, including his own *Pacifica* case, relied on three unique characteristics of the broadcast medium: the scarcity of frequencies on the electromagnetic spectrum, the long history of government regulation in allocating frequencies and ensuring that licensees acted in the public interest, and the "invasive" nature of the medium. "Those factors are not present in cyberspace," Stevens said. Agreeing with the lower court that "content on the Internet is as diverse as human thought," Stevens concluded that there is "no basis for qualifying the level of First Amendment scrutiny that should be applied to this medium." Thus, Internet speech is at least as free as speech in newspapers, in books, or on soapboxes. For government to restrict the content of online communication, it would have to prove that the restriction serves a "compelling" government interest and is narrowly tailored to serve that interest so that no less restrictive means would do.

Justice Stevens then turned to the ambiguities in the CDA statute and how they endangered free speech. He pointed to the use of "indecent" in one provision and "patently offensive" in the other, noting the lack of definition for either. These ambiguities, Stevens said, would

> provoke uncertainty among speakers about how the two standards relate to each other and just what they mean. Could a speaker confidently assume that a serious discussion about birth control practices, homosexuality, the First Amendment issues raised by the Appendix to our *Pacifica* opinion, or the consequences of prison rape would not violate the CDA? This uncertainty undermines the likelihood that the CDA has been carefully tailored to the congressional goal of protecting minors from potentially harmful materials.

The law's vagueness was troublesome for First Amendment purposes not only because the restrictions on speech were content-based but also because the CDA was a criminal law and, Stevens asserted, "The severity of criminal sanctions may well cause speakers to remain silent rather than communicate even arguably unlawful words, ideas, and images."

Justice Stevens's opinion for the Court concluded that "the CDA lacks the precision that the First Amendment requires when a statute regulates the content of speech." In trying to protect children from exposure to indecent material, the justice explained, "the CDA effectively suppresses a large amount of speech that adults have a constitutional right to receive and to address to one another." He added that government may not reduce the adult population to "only what is fit for children" and the level of Internet discourse "cannot be limited to that suitable for a sandbox."

The Court also noted that if "community standards" are used to judge offensiveness, as they are in broadcast and obscenity cases, any Internet communication, available to a nationwide audience, "will be judged by the standards of the community most likely to be offended by the message." Material at risk would include not only any of the seven dirty words used by George Carlin but also "discussions of prison rape or safe sexual practices, artistic images that include nude subjects, and arguably the card catalogue of the Carnegie Library. Also, a parent allowing her 17-year-old to use the family computer to obtain information that the parent deems appropriate, or a parent who emailed his 17-year-old college freshman information on birth control, would be subject to a lengthy prison term." Since there are less restrictive alternatives to criminal prosecution for shielding children from exposure to unwanted Internet material (such as parents installing filters, Web sites requiring credit cards for blatant sexual material, etc.), the government failed to justify the CDA's ham-handed suppression of the Internet speech of ordinary citizens.

Finally, Justice Stevens made short shrift of the government's last-ditch, desperate contention that, apart from the interest in protecting children, it had an "equally significant" interest in "fostering the growth of the Internet" as a communications medium. The government argued that the easy availability of "indecent" material on the Internet was "driving countless citizens away from the medium because of the risk of exposing themselves or their children to harmful material."

Justice Stevens responded: "The dramatic expansion of this new marketplace of ideas contradicts the factual basis of this contention . . . [as] the growth of the Internet has been and continues to be phenomenal." More importantly, as a First Amendment matter, he continued: "We presume that governmental regulation of the content of speech is more likely to interfere with the free exchange of ideas than to encourage it. The interest in encouraging freedom of expression in a democratic society outweighs any theoretical but unproven benefit of censorship." The CDA was thus swiftly interred, and the most democratic means of communication ever invented was allowed to flourish.

■　■　■

In light of *Reno v. ACLU*, Clinton Fein's case looked like a slam dunk. The Supreme Court had proclaimed that "indecent" online speech could not be made criminal, and in our case the government did not even have the supposed interest in protecting children to rely on. Instead of graciously conceding that the provision of the CDA outlawing indecent communications made with intent to annoy was unconstitutional, however, Attorney General Reno's underlings came up with a shameless "interpretation" of the law that would rescue it. For the first time in the litigation, the government said that the law did not mean what it said. It did not in fact outlaw "indecent" communications at all. The government asserted that the provision prohibiting "obscene, lewd, lascivious, filthy, *or* indecent" communications was limited to "obscene" communications.

Therefore, the government contended, because Clinton Fein was not in the business of putting obscene material online, the law did not apply to him, and his case should be dismissed.

The government's supposed "interpretation" of the statute was ridiculous. It robbed "indecent" and all the other terms of independent meaning. It was as if Congress had enacted the Communications *Obscenity* Act instead of the Communications Decency Act. It ignored the fact that the CDA used "indecent" as contrasted with "obscene" in other provisions of the same law (the provisions struck down in the *ACLU* case). As in *Pacifica* and many other decisions a clear distinction had always been made between "obscene" and "indecent" speech, and they had different meanings. Further, the government's creative exercise in statutory interpretation made the law redundant of all the other federal obscenity laws. Obscenity already was prohibited, in any medium, so the government's interpretation would render the statute meaningless.

Alas, two of the three district court judges agreed with the government. They reasoned that a court should construe a law in a way to avoid declaring it unconstitutional (a judicial restraint principle rejected in the 2010 *Citizens United* case). They referred to a few older cases that construed a "string of words" similar to those in the statute in question to mean "obscene," and they said cases like the *ACLU* case and *Pacifica* were somehow different because they involved attempts to protect minors. Their reasoning did not make any sense, but Reno's interpretation gave the judges a convenient way to avoid sticking their necks out and forthrightly declaring the law unconstitutional. The judges concluded that because Fein did not challenge the prohibition of obscenity, his case would be dismissed.

Judge Susan Illston dissented. She pointed out that the law applied to the Internet, a communications medium with hundreds of millions of users, and a criminal law like this "should mean exactly what it says, so that users will know what the rules are." She believed that, following the decision in *ACLU*, the criminal prohibition of "indecent" speech violated the First Amendment.

Since the district court decision applied only in northern California, and Fein's communications were available throughout the nation, he remained at risk of prosecution in other districts, where courts might read the law to mean what it said, covering nonobscene material. Fein and all Internet users would live under the uncertain cloud of a law that on its face made "indecent" annoying communications a felony. So we took the case on a direct appeal to the Supreme Court. On April 19, 1999, the Court handed down what had to be the shortest First Amendment decision ever made: "The judgment is affirmed." No explanation. This outcome was terribly disappointing and a waste of several years of litigation during which the government had never suggested construing the law to prohibit only obscenity.

The decision had a sliver of a silver lining. The Supreme Court's action had the effect of making the district court's interpretation binding nationally. It was now the law of the land. In practical terms, therefore, the litigation gave Clinton Fein what he sought: the ability to communicate nonobscene material that might be considered indecent in some communities and to annoy the recipients without fear of criminal prosecution. He deserved but did not get a ringing affirmation that the CDA provision that threatened annoy.com violated the First Amendment.

■   ■   ■

Congress could not resist the temptation to exploit the CDA's demise politically by trying again to shield America's children from sexual material on the Internet. It promptly passed a new law, which we called "Son of CDA." The law's proper name was the Child Online Protection Act, or COPA. Congress attempted to patch up some of the constitutional deficiencies that Justice Stevens had identified in the CDA. It made three main changes from the CDA: COPA outlawed only communications made "for commercial purposes"; it was limited to communications on the World Wide Web, as opposed to the entire Internet including email; and instead of proscribing "indecent" material, it criminalized material that is "harmful to minors." Included was a laughable definition of "harmful to minors." In a parody of the three-part *Miller* definition of obscenity, COPA simply tacked on to each of the three parts something about minors. So the material must appeal to the prurient interest "with respect to minors," must be patently offensive under community standards "with respect to minors," and must lack literary or other societal value "for minors." If the *Miller* obscenity definition was subjective and vague, the COPA statute compounded these vices. Adding in all the references to minors really would have reduced Internet discourse to the lowest common denominator, because if material might not be suitable for a toddler—even though unremarkable for a sophisticated 17-year-old—it would be illegal, since both are minors.

Once again the ACLU sued the very day the law was to take effect. Once again the lower courts condemned the law. The reach of COPA admittedly was narrower than the CDA. Congress may have been targeting commercial pornographers, but the law it wrote was much broader. It still prohibited speech that is protected among adults, and it still provided no clear guidance to Web communicators who wished to avoid crossing the invisible line into criminal behavior. The court of appeals was especially concerned about COPA's use of "community standards" for judging the offensiveness of material harmful to minors, which was lifted from the *Miller* test. The court noted that material posted on the Web "is accessible by all Internet users worldwide," and Web publishers cannot restrict access to their sites based on where the users are. Therefore, the court said, COPA requires every Web publisher to "abide by the most restrictive and conservative state's community standards" to avoid criminal liability. The court of appeals threw out COPA on that ground alone.

The government of course appealed to the Supreme Court. On May 13, 2002, the Court vacated the court of appeals' decision. The Court's opinion was written by Justice Clarence Thomas, no friend of the First Amendment. The Court decided that the use of community standards to identify the prohibited material did not *by itself* make COPA unconstitutional. Justice Thomas pointed out that COPA applied to less material than the CDA and its definition of the forbidden material was narrower because it required the government to prove appeal to the prurient interest and no redeeming social value for minors. Responding to the contention that Web publishers could not control where their material might be accessed, Justice Thomas gave them some blunt advice: "If a publisher wishes for its material to be judged only by the standards of particular communities, then it need only take the simple step of utilizing a medium that enables it to target the release of its material into those communities." In other words, Web publishers shouldn't be Web publishers; they should go into the newspaper, magazine, or radio business. (This suggestion contradicts what the Court held in the CDA case when the government made a similar argument and Justice Stevens responded that this was "equivalent to arguing that a statute could ban leaflets on certain subjects as long as individuals are free to publish books"; where a restriction on speech is content-based, it is no answer to say that some other medium might be used.)

Justice Thomas candidly confessed the real reason for vacating the lower court's condemnation of COPA: "If we were to hold COPA unconstitutional because of its use of community standards, federal obscenity statutes would likely also be unconstitutional as applied to the Web." In other words, obscenity would be allowed on the Web but not in any other medium, and the Court could not countenance that result. Having so concluded, the Court sent the case back to the court of appeals for another look, to consider whether COPA was unconstitutional for some reason other than its invocation of community standards.

The court of appeals got the message and found that COPA violated the First Amendment because of its vagueness and overbreadth. The government of course appealed again. On June 29, 2004, the Supreme Court upheld the lower court's grant of a temporary injunction against enforcing COPA. This time the opinion was authored by Justice Anthony Kennedy, who perhaps surprisingly is quite consistently sensitive to First Amendment values. He began by noting that "content-based prohibitions, enforced by severe criminal penalties, have the constant potential to be a repressive force in the lives and thoughts of a free people," that these restrictions on speech are "presumed invalid," and the government has the burden of demonstrating their constitutionality. Justice Kennedy concluded that the government had not shown that less restrictive alternatives to criminal prosecution—like filtering software installed by concerned parents—could be as effective in protecting children from exposure to potentially harmful material. The court remanded the case to the lower courts for further "proceedings" to determine whether the temporary injunction should be made permanent.

Justice Stevens concurred, reaffirming his belief that "Government may not penalize speakers for making available to the general World Wide Web audience that which the least tolerant communities in America deem unfit for their children's consumption." Having struggled with restrictions on sexual speech in several cases over the years, he also took the occasion to venture his conviction that criminal prosecutions are an inappropriate means of regulating even obscene material, as the line between communications that "offend" and those that do not "is too blurred to identify criminal conduct."

Justice Stephen Breyer, who perhaps surprisingly is too apt to compromise on First Amendment issues, dissented. He thought filtering software was faulty and allowed some pornographic material to pass through without hindrance: "The software alone cannot distinguish between the most obscene pictorial image and the Venus de Milo." He also despaired that "After eight years of legislative effort, two statutes, and three Supreme Court cases, the Court sends this case back to the district court for further proceedings." Breyer thought Congress had tried hard enough to repair the defects in the CDA, and the COPA was good enough. He threw up his hands and said, literally, "What else was Congress supposed to do?"

Back in the district court in Pennsylvania, the judge conducted a trial, giving the government the opportunity to show that there were no less restrictive alternatives to criminal prosecution under COPA that could protect children. Judge Lowell Reed found, however, that filters were more effective than COPA's criminal prohibitions. He pointed out that perhaps half of sexually explicit Web sites are foreign in origin and that it is practically impossible to prosecute them in the United States, while filters can screen at least some of their material. He found COPA both under-inclusive (in not being able to do anything about foreign Web sites) and over-inclusive (in deeming material unlawful if it might be harmful for a five-year-old even though it would be unobjectionable for a sophisticated teenager), and therefore not "narrowly tailored" to serve the interest in protecting children. Judge Reed concluded that "I may not turn a blind eye to the law in order to satisfy my urge to protect this nation's youth by upholding a flawed statute. . . . Perhaps we do the minors of this country harm if First Amendment protections, which they will with age inherit fully, are chipped away in the name of their protection."

The government of course appealed again. It argued that the First Amendment "does not prevent Congress from adopting a 'belt-and-suspenders' approach . . . with filters acting as the 'belt' and COPA [criminal prosecution] as the 'suspenders.'" The court responded: "Under the First Amendment, if the belt works at least as effectively as the suspenders, then the government cannot prosecute people for not wearing suspenders."

By this time the government was bring represented by attorney general Michael Mukasey (President George W. Bush's successor to Alberto Gonzales), who tried to take the case to the Supreme Court for the third time. On January 21, 2009, the Court denied review. COPA was dead. It, like CDA, never took effect.

■   ■   ■

Congress made another attempt to restrict sexual content on the Internet. The Child Pornography Prevention Act of 1996 (CPPA) amended the federal child pornography law to make it a crime to possess or distribute pictures not just of real children but of what "appear to be" minors in sexual poses. Congress said that computer-generated images, even those that do not involve real children at all in their production, should be prohibited because such pictures might be used to "whet the appetite" of pedophiles or be used by child abusers to seduce their victims. This was a new rationale for outlawing child pornography. The Supreme Court had approved laws outlawing pictures of minors performing sex acts because of the child abuse inherent in the *production* of the pictures, without requiring that the pictures themselves be legally obscene.

The CPPA was challenged by a group of "adult" entertainment businesses, a publisher of nudist books, a painter of nudes, and a photographer specializing in erotic images, who called themselves the Free Speech Coalition. They won in the lower court, and of course the government took the case to the Supreme Court. I wrote an *amicus curiae* brief for the ACLU and several other organizations. Justice Kennedy wrote a courageous opinion, reaffirming vital First Amendment principles in an unsavory context. One of the problems with CPPA, Justice Kennedy found, was that it outlawed not just computer-generated images but also "a renaissance painting depicting a scene from classical mythology" as well as Hollywood movies like *Lolita*, *Traffic*, and *American Beauty*, in which young-looking adult actors (who appear to be minors) are seen engaging in sexual acts. It also covered pictures in a psychology manual and a documentary "depicting the horrors of sexual abuse." In other words, the CPPA outlawed a range of images of significant societal value even though *no real children* were used in their production.

Justice Kennedy acknowledged that "sexual abuse of a child is a most serious crime," and Congress has the power to protect children from abuse, but he contended, "The prospect of crime . . . by itself does not justify laws suppressing protected speech." Repeating a lesson learned in *Hustler v. Falwell*, Kennedy said: "Speech may not be prohibited because it concerns subjects offending our sensibilities." The justice was especially troubled that, in the absence of the *Miller* obscenity requirement—material must lack literary, artistic, or other value to be deemed obscene—works of art and movies could be condemned "without inquiry into the work's redeeming value." Moreover, he said, the CPPA prohibits "the visual depiction of an idea—that of teenagers engaging in sexual activity—that is a fact of modern society and has been a theme of art and literature throughout the ages."

As for the government's argument that even virtual images could lead to actual child abuse, Justice Kennedy first noted that "the causal link is contingent and indirect." That is, the connection between viewing child porn and actually molesting kids is not clear. (Indeed, the social science research does not establish a causal link between viewing any kind of pornography and sexual crime.) Also, cartoons, video games, and candy might be used to seduce children, yet Kennedy points out: "We would not expect those to be prohibited because they can be misused." More fundamentally, the government's "whet-the-appetite" contention runs afoul of the First Amendment principle that "the mere tendency of speech to encourage unlawful acts is not a sufficient reason for banning it." The CPPA was basically aimed at the evil of planting bad ideas and impure thoughts, but government is not allowed to control thought. Justice Kennedy reminded everyone of *Brandenburg v. Ohio*: even "advocacy" of illegal conduct and hateful ideas is protected unless it amounts to incitement of imminent lawless acts. The CPPA, like the CDA and the COPA, was dead.

■   ■   ■

Congress finally found limited success in attempting to regulate sexual content on the Internet when, on June 23, 2003, the Supreme Court upheld a fourth law, the Children's Internet Protection Act (CIPA). The law denies federal funding to public libraries unless they have a "policy of Internet safety for minors" that uses software filters to prevent access by anyone to "visual depictions" that are "harmful to minors." The statute, sponsored by Senator John McCain, does not define any of these terms.

Chief Justice Rehnquist wrote the Court's opinion in the ominously named case, *United States v. American Library Association*. The Court emphasized that this law, unlike CDA and COPA, did not impose any criminal sanctions and, importantly: "Congress has wide latitude to attach conditions to the receipt of federal assistance." In other words, the government is not required to fund libraries and can put strings on the subsidies it chooses to make. Rehnquist stated that libraries are free to offer unfiltered access "without federal assistance" and CIPA "is a valid exercise of Congress's spending power."

The Court understood that filters notoriously over-block, screening out material that is completely innocuous as well as valuable, such as the Carlin monologue or the syllabus for a university course on sex education. Asked at the oral argument whether the law would prevent adult users of library computers from access to such material, the government lawyer told the Court that a librarian would unblock any given site or disable the filter at the request of an adult user. On the basis of this unrealistically optimistic representation, the Court concluded that adult access to the full resources of the Internet would not be unduly hindered. Two justices concurred in the decision only because of this representation, making a majority upholding the law. Justice Stevens, in dissent, was unpersuaded by the government's assurance and said the law was tantamount to requiring a library's materials to be kept in "unmarked, locked rooms or cabinets, which could be opened only in response to specific requests." More broadly, Stevens reasoned that a law's abridgement of speech "is equally obnoxious" whether it is enforced by "a threat of penalties or by a threat to withhold a benefit."

■   ■   ■

Whether software filters solve First Amendment Internet problems is an amusing diversion. In the library case, the government urged that filters are effective in protecting children from exposure to harmful material, while civil libertarians argued that they over-block and under-block, and that government has no business policing libraries anyway. In the CDA and COPA cases, the roles were reversed. The ACLU argued that filters were effective, and that children could be protected by less restrictive means than criminal prosecutions, while the government urged that filters were ineffective and the criminal sanction was needed. The seeming inconsistency was nicely resolved by Ann Beeson of the ACLU, who said the central issue is whose finger is on the mouse, the government's or the parent's: "When a parent installs a filter that keeps a kid from seeing a bunch of sites that may or may not be pornography, that's parenting. When a government forces all adults and minors to use filters, that's censorship."

The broader issue in all this is whether the courts should accept the government's assertion that it has a "compelling" interest in protecting minors from being exposed to material that it deems harmful. So far, the courts have uncritically accepted this proposition in case after case and then have wrestled with whether the particular speech restriction is "narrowly tailored" to serve the asserted interest. They have done so without any evidence that the supposedly harmful material actually causes any harm. That is, the government has not been required to prove that minors are in fact injured in any way by hearing dirty words or seeing sexual images. This has allowed politicians to enact laws that restrict everyone's speech in the name of protecting children. This cause is seductive and dangerous because the principle has no limits. If we uncritically accept that the government has a compelling interest in shielding children from various kinds of speech that it deems harmful, there is nothing to prevent legislators from enacting a Newspaper Decency Act, a Literature Decency Act, or laws banning profanity, Facebook, or bad grammar.

■   ■   ■

Having survived the CDA and the COPA, Clinton Fein continued to annoy various people with his digital muckraking and provocative images. Annoy.com had another run-in with the Justice Department. Unbeknownst to Fein, someone used annoy.com's postcard service anonymously to send a threatening message to a university administrator in Houston. Out of the blue, without notice or opportunity to be heard, Fein was served with a court order issued by a federal magistrate in Houston, commanding the site to disclose the identity of the user. The order also prohibited Fein from disclosing the existence of *the order* to the user "or to any other person." Fein responded by informing the government that he had no information about the identity of the anonymous user *and* by moving to quash the "gag" provision as an unconstitutional prior restraint on his free speech. The lower court refused to lift the nondisclosure order so that Fein could discuss publicly the propriety of the government's obtaining secret orders demanding that Web sites surrender user information. We had to appeal to the Fifth Circuit Court of Appeals. That court noted that the law the government had invoked authorized nondisclosure orders only to protect life or physical safety and only for a limited period, and it sent the case back to the lower court to consider the "substantial constitutional questions" raised by its order. The lower court then vacated the order and, of course, annoy.com covered the controversy.

■   ■   ■

Clinton Fein's other brush with the legal system found the ACLU, long the guardian of First Amendment freedom, not in a heroic role. In an employment discrimination suit against Avis Rent a Car at the San Francisco airport, three Latino workers proved that they had been subjected to verbal harassment by one supervisor. By way of relief, a California Court of Appeal directed that the trial court compile a list of "prohibited epithets," the use of which the company would be enjoined from allowing in the workplace. The record in the case did not disclose what disparaging names the workers had been called or the context in which they were used, but the court required the promulgation of a list of government-forbidden words that could not be uttered in the workplace.

Momentarily blinded by some notion of political correctness, the ACLU supported the order and argued to the California Supreme Court that it should be affirmed. It said that a proven pattern of workplace hostility justified an injunction against using government-prescribed bad words in the future. That is, a competing value—the need to remedy employment discrimination—trumped free-speech considerations. Clinton Fein, ever alert to diminution of First Amendment freedoms, disagreed. So we tendered an *amicus curiae* brief to the California Supreme Court.

We argued that "The First Amendment does not say government 'shall make no law abridging the freedom of speech, except to protect certain persons from ridicule and insult in the workplace.'" We urged that words in the abstract cannot be made unlawful or enjoined. Meaning depends on context. For example, to take the most famous racial slur, uttering the word "nigger" may be a sign of friendship and intimacy, or of bigotry and hate, depending on the context—to whom it is said, by whom, in what tone of voice, and in what circumstances. As

Supreme Court Justice John Marshall Harlan once said: "One man's vulgarity is another's lyric." The same is true of whatever epithets would be on the court's list. If "spic" were on the list, the injunction would prohibit both screaming at a Latino subordinate: "You fucking lazy spic!" and saying discreetly to a peer: "I believe it is a violation of the First Amendment for a court to issue an injunction forbidding me from saying 'spic' to anyone." To say that there is no legal difference between these two is to say that context is irrelevant and that government can outlaw the mere utterance of disfavored words.

Even though courts may award damages to victims of workplace discrimination who have been subjected to abusive language, that does not mean, we argued, that a court can issue an injunction against future offensive speech. A government order that specific speech may not be uttered would be an impermissible prior restraint on speech. Orders prohibiting speech in advance have always been constitutionally suspect. The point is that speech is protected until it can be shown to have done actual harm. One of the chief purposes of the First Amendment is to prevent prior restraints. They can be granted only in the most exceptional circumstances, such as immediate threats to the national security. In the *Pentagon Papers* case, the U.S. Supreme Court found that the government had failed to prove sufficient harm to national security to justify a prior restraint.

Alas, the California Supreme Court, doubtless lulled by assurances from none other than the First Amendment champion ACLU that it should not worry about free-speech considerations in remedying employment discrimination, and quoting the ACLU brief, approved the concept of an injunction against uttering any "prohibited epithets." However, the court ducked the issue of whether courts should compile lists of forbidden words, saying that since the parties had not "sought review" of that issue, the court would express "no opinion" on it. The court left it to the lower court to fashion an order telling employees what they are permitted to say about other employees.

■   ■   ■

Undaunted by his encounters with the legal system, Clinton Fein continues to rail against politicians and powerful corporations, using both annoy.com and art. He has become a digital artist of some renown and is a direct beneficiary of *Hustler v. Falwell* and its protection for offensive satire. Working with a computer, Photoshop software, and a digital camera, Fein has created political "cartoons," collages, and other images that offend their targets and many others. His work has been widely published and has appeared in art galleries, but not without controversy. The headline of a review in the *San Francisco Chronicle* states plainly: "His art is not subtle. It can be hard to take. But Clinton Fein is not afraid to make a statement." Shortly after the 9/11 attacks, Fein had a show at a San Francisco gallery. The magazine *Artforum* refused to run an advertisement for the show. The ad, one of Fein's images, showed former New York mayor Rudy Giuliani sitting naked in a urine-filled glass (reminiscent of a Damien Hirst work), referencing Giuliani's retaliatory withholding of funding for the Brooklyn Museum.

Fein savagely attacked the George W. Bush administration at every opportunity, especially the invasion of Iraq and the Abu Ghraib torture. One of his images shows the president nailed to the cross crucifixion-style, with an erection popping out of his loincloth in the shape of a rocket, under the banner "Who Would Jesus Torture?" Another looks to a casual viewer like an American flag, but in the background of each stripe is the text of the Taguba Report on the Abu Ghraib torture, and the "stars" are whitened images of the iconic photograph of the hooded and wired torturee. For an art gallery show, Fein sent the images to a large format printer in Palo Alto, Zazzle. The printer found the images offensive and destroyed them. This sort of censorship does not violate the First Amendment, of course, because only the government is bound by and can violate the Constitution.

Nor does it dampen Fein's willingness fully to exercise the freedom of expression that brought him to America. His imagery is sometimes sexual and includes anuses, erect penises, and Carlinesque words describing them. He says his mother "wishes [he] would do watercolors." But his work is not pornographic and certainly not obscene, even though right-wing groups call him a "noted homosexual pornographer." His work does not appeal to the prurient interest, and it clearly has political and artistic value. A First Amendment true believer, he indefatigably tries to expose hypocrisy, skewer the mainstream media for laziness and cowardice, and provoke debate over accepted wisdom. But this defender of online freedom also laments young people's willingness to give up any semblance of privacy on Facebook and other social networking sites, so that "Nothing [is] left for anyone to discover about you. Government doesn't have to spy; they can just join Facebook."

AFTERWORD

Among the lessons to be drawn from the adventures of our heroes and villains are these two: we have to be skeptical of the government's arguments that competing values require restrictions on speech, and we don't need a new First Amendment for the 21st century.

The government doesn't get the benefit of the doubt

We—and particularly the courts—should not uncritically accept the government's supposed justifications for restricting speech. As we have seen, the government always argues that some competing value supports limitations on speech or press freedoms. But notice a disturbing pattern in the stories of First Amendment heroism and villainy: in so many instances the government cried wolf or, at least, exaggerated the calamities that would befall the country if certain speech were not suppressed. In some cases, we saw that the government even deceived the courts. For example, from Dannie Martin's trial we learned that the Federal Bureau of Prisons was defending its no-interview rule as essential to prison security even though it already had determined the rule was not needed, and it abandoned the rule soon after winning its point in the Supreme Court. In Earl Caldwell's case, it turned out that the government did not need his testimony at all and dropped the matter as soon as it persuaded the Supreme Court that his testimony was crucial to law enforcement. In Yetta Stromberg's case, where the officials urged that outlawing display of a red flag was necessary to preserve "organized government" against a Bolshevik takeover, time showed that this was fantasy. In the Jehovah's Witnesses cases, arguments that during wartime "national unity" required schoolchildren to recite the Pledge of Allegiance proved empty. In the Communications Decency Act case, the government's argument that pornography would ruin the Internet for everyone blinked reality. In the landmark Pentagon Papers controversy, the government's dire prediction that the nation would suffer grave harm from their publication proved baseless.

In short, we and the courts should aim a healthy skepticism toward whatever claims the government makes to justify speech suppression. Harm can never be assumed. The government must always be put to its proof. That may involve risk, but freedom is not risk-free. As President Obama said of national security in his inaugural address, "We reject as false the choice between our safety and our ideals." Every nation wants and legitimately tries to ensure its safety. But our ideals define who we are as a nation; our ideals, especially our First Amendment freedoms, *are* our safety.

Don't amend the Constitution

Encounters like those of Clinton Fein with restrictions on digital speech raise the question whether our antique First Amendment, written in 1789, is up to the task of dealing with 21st-century communications. James Madison would have had a hard time getting his mind around instant worldwide Internet speech. In the early days of the digital era, some thoughtful observers of the new technology, conscious of its democratizing potential, proposed a constitutional amendment to ensure cyberspace freedom. Harvard Law Professor Laurence Tribe, for example, advocated amending the Constitution to say: "Protections for freedoms of speech, press [and other constitutional rights] . . . shall be construed as fully applicable without regard to the technological method or medium through which information content is generated, stored, altered, transmitted, or controlled." More recently, in response to the 2010 *Citizens United* decision, organizations like ReclaimDemocracy.org proposed amending the Constitution to eliminate free-speech rights for corporations or, more generally, to restrict corporate "personhood."

I don't think it's a good idea to tinker with the Bill of Rights. Amending the source of our fundamental freedoms is a perilous undertaking with an uncertain outcome. Opening up the amendment process would unleash pressures to include provisions on school prayer, flag burning, and who knows what else. In my view, we don't need a new First Amendment. The creaky old document, as interpreted over the years, has made us a free people and is flexible enough to protect our freedoms in any century.

To be sure, the Supreme Court has often distinguished among communications media, saying that "differences in the characteristics of new media justify differences in the First Amendment standards applied to them." The Court has in fact applied the First Amendment differently depending on the media involved: television, radio, newspapers, and the Internet. For example, in 1969 the Court upheld the Fairness Doctrine developed by the FCC. The Doctrine originated in the early days of radio in the 1920s and governed FCC-licensed radio and television broadcasters. It required them to act in the public interest by covering important issues of the day and by giving voice to contrasting views on the issues. The FCC also developed a "personal attack" rule, requiring broadcasters whose programs attacked a person's honesty or integrity to allow the person to respond to the attack. The Fairness Doctrine and the personal-attack rule were upheld in *Red Lion v. FCC*. As in the Jehovah's Witnesses cases, the broadcasters claimed a First Amendment right not to speak, a right not to be forced to give voice to views with which they disagreed. The Court disagreed, saying, "It is the right of the viewers and listeners . . . which is paramount."

Just five years later, the Court treated a very similar issue completely differently with regard to newspapers. In *Miami Herald v. Tornillo*, the Court held that a Florida law giving a "right of reply" to political candidates who were attacked by a newspaper violated the First Amendment. The Court recognized the growing concentration of ownership of newspapers in the hands of powerful corporations—many cities have only one paper—and the homogeneity of views that this engenders. It also acknowledged the candidates' contention that "the 'marketplace of ideas' is today a monopoly controlled by the owners of the market." But the Court refused to allow government to require that newspapers include certain government-specified content. (My thought: a press that government requires to be fair is not free.) The only way *Red Lion* and *Miami Herald* can be reconciled and happily coexist in the same jurisprudential universe is to accept that the differences in the characteristics of the media—broadcast and print—justify different First Amendment rules.

Fortunately, in the Communications Decency Act case, the Court rejected the government's contention that the Internet should be treated as broadcast media, not print. The Court decided the Internet should be at least as free from government control as newspapers. It actually should be freer, given the unique characteristics of digital communication: it is cheap, interactive, user-controlled, and democratic, and it lets us all be publishers. All of the First Amendment principles reaffirmed by the Court in the infamous *Citizens United* decision fully apply to—and protect—the Internet medium. Amending the Constitution is not needed to ensure 21st-century freedom.

Citizens United redux

But what about amending it to limit corporate "personhood" and end First Amendment protection for corporate speech? The Court in *Red Lion* limited the First Amendment rights of some powerful corporations—licensed broadcasters—in the name of facilitating the interest of all citizens in *receiving* a diversity of views. (The Fairness Doctrine itself was abandoned in 1987 by the Reagan-era FCC as an unnecessary regulation on business. Periodically attempts are made in Congress to resuscitate the doctrine. Recently these attempts have met with vociferous opposition from the Christian right, which protests that "liberals" want to shut down talk-radio titans like Rush Limbaugh—who give no voice to opposing views—by enacting what they call "The Silence Christian and Conservative Broadcasters Law.")

The Court in *Citizens United* invoked the same idea—the public's right to receive information—as a justification for permitting corporate political speech: we citizens are entitled to hear political speech from whatever source because the First Amendment protects political *speech* regardless of the identity of the speaker.

But the Court's finding that corporate "persons" are constitutionally empowered to speak was not firmly rooted in either history or public policy. Did the framers of the Constitution intend to include corporations along with natural persons as having the right to free speech? This question of the "original understanding" resulted in a pissing match between Justice Antonin Scalia and Justice John Paul Stevens. Probably to tweak the noses of Scalia, Justice Clarence Thomas, and other "originalists" (those who contend that the Constitution should be interpreted to mean what its framers understood it to mean), Stevens devoted a whole section of his dissent to "Original Understandings." Stevens noted 18th-century fears of "soulless" business corporations and quoted Thomas Jefferson's "hope" to "crush . . . the aristocracy of our monied corporations which dare already to challenge our government to a trial of strength and bid defiance to the laws of our country." Based on the historical evidence he could marshal, Stevens asserted that when the framers wrote the First Amendment, "It was the free speech of individual Americans they had in mind . . . [and they] . . . took it as a given that corporations could be comprehensively regulated in the service of the public welfare." Stevens emphasized that corporations are different from individual speakers and should not be treated identically to natural persons. After all, these artificial beings have perpetual life, limited liability, and favorable tax treatment enabling the accumulation of assets. Stevens concluded that they have "no consciences, no beliefs, no feelings, no thoughts, no desires. . . . They are not themselves members of 'We the People' by whom and for whom our Constitution was established."

This provoked Justice Scalia to write a separate concurring opinion supporting the Court's recognition of corporate free speech. Scalia noted that the *text* of the First Amendment makes no distinction between types of speakers and complained that the dissent found not "even an isolated statement from the founding era to the effect that corporations are *not* covered." Scalia acknowledged that statesmen from the founding era distrusted corporations but said, "Most of the Founders' resentment towards corporations was directed at the state-granted monopoly privileges [that corporations then enjoyed]. . . . Modern corporations do not have such privileges, and would probably have been favored by most of our enterprising Founders—excluding, perhaps, Thomas Jefferson and others favoring perpetuation of an agrarian society." In a final, triumphant pro-corporate flourish, Scalia concluded that "to exclude or impede corporate speech is to muzzle the principal agents of the modern free economy. We should celebrate rather than condemn the addition of this speech to the public debate."

Stevens in turn responded that Scalia had failed to come up with founding era statements that the framers meant to *include* corporate speakers within the First Amendment protections. The disagreement was a standoff; neither side was able to point to contemporaneous statements or specific historical evidence demonstrating the framers' actual intent. Apparently we will never know what they had in mind, though it seems highly unlikely that the framers wanted the corporations they mistrusted (which were then specially chartered by state legislatures) to have the same speech rights as individuals.

We do know that according corporations constitutional rights like those of real persons crept into the Supreme Court's jurisprudence as a historical fluke and without any real analysis. In an 1886 railroad case, *Santa Clara County v. Southern Pacific*, the Court simply assumed that the railroad was a "person" protected by the Equal Protection Clause of the then-new Fourteenth Amendment and refused to hear argument on the question. By 1898, the Court was able casually to say, again without any analysis, that whether corporations are persons under the Equal Protection Clause was "settled." (This, despite the text of the amendment: It uses "person" five times and the context clearly demonstrates that it meant natural persons. For example, persons "born or naturalized" in the United States are citizens, representatives are apportioned among states according to the number of persons excluding "Indians not taxed," and persons are barred from holding office if they engaged in rebellion.) The Court also decided long ago that the *Fifth* Amendment privilege against self-incrimination, which also belongs to a "person," is "essentially a personal one, applying only to natural individuals."

The Court has never squarely confronted or carefully analyzed whether corporations should have the same free-speech rights as natural persons. The treatment of corporations as persons with constitutional rights has been inconsistent, unexplained, and baffling, and it is in need of some serious attention.

Justice Kennedy's opinion for the Court said, "The Court has recognized that First Amendment protection extends to corporations." To support this proposition, Kennedy cited 24 important First Amendment decisions going back several decades, all of which involved speech by corporations. They included such landmarks as *New York Times v. Sullivan* and the *Pentagon Papers* case, which guaranteed the rights to criticize government and to be free of prior restraints on speech.

It seems too late in the day to roll back the clock and say that corporations have no First Amendment rights. No one would want to say that the *New York Times* or CBS News has no First Amendment protection and is, therefore, subject to unbridled government censorship. Many of the most important free-speech rights we all enjoy were won in cases involving corporate speech.

However, it is not too late to determine that corporations have more limited speech rights than individuals, and that their executives can reasonably be restricted from spending money that is not their own on elections. The law need not treat corporations like soapbox orators and pamphleteers and can treat them as having more restricted rights than natural persons. The Court in *Citizens United* acknowledged that some speakers—public school students, prisoners, persons on military bases, and government employees—do not enjoy full First Amendment protection even for core political speech.

Why corporations should have rights superior to these groups is unclear. The Court has also determined (in *Red Lion*) that broadcasting corporations do not have the same right *not* to speak as Jehovah's Witnesses (in the flag salute and license plate cases). In other words, ample precedent exists for giving corporate speech less protection than the speech of natural persons.

In fact, *Citizens United* did not decide that corporate speech rights are *identical* to those of natural persons. Why not say that because corporations are very different beings, they are subject to differential treatment and their speech is subject to reasonable limitations? The overbroad and somewhat clumsy law thrown out in *Citizens United* might not have been a reasonable and carefully tailored restriction on what corporations can do to influence elections. But *Citizens United* is probably not the last word on this subject. A thorough reexamination of the nature of corporations and the extent to which they can claim the benefits of the Bill of Rights would be timely. Is there some good reason why corporations are not allowed to vote and do not have a Fifth Amendment privilege against self-incrimination but do have a First Amendment right to speak? If they do have free-speech rights, why should they be identical to those of natural persons?

．　　．　　．

It's a shame that the wonderful First Amendment principles recited and reinforced in *Citizens United* benefited corporations rather than otherwise powerless individuals challenging entrenched power. One can only hope that in the future the principles will be invoked to protect genuine First Amendment heroes.

NOTES

Transcripts of court proceedings and sources for quotations are on file with the author. Citations to the cases and other published sources follow:

Introduction

3   *A recent study found that only half of high school students:* "First Amendment No Big Deal, Students Say: Study Shows American Teenagers Indifferent to Freedoms," *Associated Press*, January 31, 2005. http://msnbc.msn.com/id/6888837/.

3   *Supreme Court Justice Sandra Day O'Connor:* "Former Justice Promotes Web-Based Civics Lessons," *New York Times*, June 9, 2008, p. B7.

4   *Bill Clinton once said: New York Times*, December 17, 1997, p. A17.

5   *Sarah Palin got it upside down:* Glenn Greenwald, "Sarah Palin Speaks on the First Amendment," Salon.com, October 8, 2008. http://salon.com/opinion/greenwald/2008/10/31/palin.

6   *The Supreme Court's 2010 decision on corporate speech: Citizens United v. Federal Election Commission*, 558 U.S. ___ (2010).

6   *printed a nearly hysterical editorial:* "The Court's Blow to Democracy," *New York Times*, January 22, 2010.

7   *People for the American Way:* People for the American Way direct mail solicitation, February, 2010.

8   Bush v. Gore: *Bush v. Gore*, 531 U.S. 98 (2000).

9   Buckley v. Valeo: *Buckley v. Valeo*, 424 U.S. 1 (1976).

12   Whitney v. California: *Whitney v. California*, 274 U.S. 357 (1927).

13   Near v. Minnesota: *Near v. Minnesota*, 283 U.S. 687 (1931).

14   *the very same five-justice majority intervened:* Hollingsworth v. Perry, 558 U.S. ____ (2010).

1. Yetta Stromberg

17   *a summer camp for young Communists:* American Civil Liberties Union, *The California Red Flag Case* (1930). The ACLU pamphlet, seeking funds for the appeal of Yetta Stromberg's case, lays out many of the facts from the time of trial.

18   *The Federation . . . believed the republic was being undermined:* Kevin Starr, *Endangered Dreams*, p. 156 (1997).

19   *Kate Crane Gartz . . . wrote Judge Allison a letter:* Lauren Coodley, ed., *The Land of Orange Groves and Jails: Upton Sinclair's California*, p. 89–90 (2004).

20   *On May 18, 1931, the Court handed down its decision:* Stromberg v. California, 283 U.S. 359 (1931).

21   Gitlow v. New York: *Gitlow v. New York*, 268 U.S. 652 (1925).

22   New York Times v. Sullivan: *New York Times v. Sullivan*, 376 U.S. 254 (1964).

23   *David Paul O'Brien burned his draft card:* United States v. O'Brien, 391 U.S. 367 (1968).

24   *When high school students in Des Moines wore black armbands:* Tinker v. Des Moines Independent Community School District, 393 U.S. 503 (1969).

24   *When Gregory Lee Johnson burned an American flag:* Texas v. Johnson, 491 U.S. 397 (1989).

25   *Court, in a surprising opinion by Justice Antonin Scalia:* R.A.V. v. City of St. Paul, 505 U.S. 377 (1992).

25   *Chief Justice Roberts found . . . the banner conveyed the wrong message:* Morse v. Frederick, 551 U.S. 393 (2007).

2. Jehovah's Witnesses

28   *"believe in the Bible as the Word of God"*: Jehovah's Witnesses, "Who Are They?" Jehovah's Witnesses Official Web site. http://watchtower.org/e/jt/article_01.htm (2009).

28   *The Supreme Court reversed Lovell's conviction: Lovell v. Griffin*, 333 U.S. 444 (1938).

30   Cantwell v. Connecticut: *Cantwell v. Connecticut*, 310 U.S. 296 (1940).

30   *The Supreme Court stepped in and taught a few civics lessons: West Virginia Board of Education v. Barnette*, 319 U.S. 624 (1943).

33   *a more recent Jehovah's Witnesses case: Wooley v. Maynard*, 430 U.S. 705 (1977).

34   *Twenty or so states now offer:* Adam Liptak, "Is That Plate Speaking for the Driver or the State?" *New York Times*, April 28, 2009.

35   *The Supreme Court upheld the conviction: Chaplinsky v. New Hampshire*, 315 U.S. 568 (1942).

37   *the Court's three-part definition:* see *Miller v. California*, 413 U.S. 15 (1973) and discussion in Chapter 8.

37   New York Times v. Sullivan: *New York Times v. Sullivan*, 376 U.S. 254 (1964).

37   *unprotected category of child pornography: Ashcroft v. Free Speech Coalition*, 535 U.S. 234 (2002).

37   *the Court rejected the government's claim that depictions of animal cruelty: United States v. Stevens*, 558 U.S. ____ (2010).

39   *June 14, 1943, in the midst of war: Taylor v. Mississippi*, 319 U.S. 583 (1943).

39   Schenck v. United States: *Schenck v. United States*, 249 U.S. 47 (1919).

40   *the Court upheld the conviction of Eugene Debs: Debs v. United States*, 249 U.S. 211 (1919).

40   Abrams v. United States: *Abrams v. United States*, 250 U.S. 616 (1919).

41   Whitney v. California: *Whitney v. California*, 274 U.S. 357 (1927).

41   *the Court upheld the convictions of Communists: Dennis v. United States*, 341 U.S. 494 (1951).

41   *While . . . the Court seems to have abandoned clear and present danger:* see *Brandenburg v. Ohio*, 395 U.S. 444 (1969), and the discussion in Chapter 7.

42   *One of Yoo's infamous memoranda:* John C. Yoo and Robert J. Delahunty, Memorandum for Alberto Gonzales, Counsel for the President, *Authority for Use of Military Force to Combat Terrorist Activities Within the United States*, p. 24 (October 23, 2001).

42   *President Barack Obama's declaration:* President Barack Obama, Inauguration Speech (January 20, 2009).

42   *the Witnesses' most recent visit to the Supreme Court: Watchtower Bible and Tract Society v. Village of Stratton*, 536 U.S. 150 (2002).

3. Dannie Martin

45   *So said Dannie Martin:* Dannie M. Martin and Peter Y. Sussman, *Committing Journalism: The Prison Writings of Red Hog* (1993).

46   *"Requiem for Mr. Squirrel":* "Requiem for Mr. Squirrel," *Committing Journalism*, p. 50 (1993).

46   *the* Chronicle *published Martin's "The Gulag Mentality":* "The Gulag Mentality," *Committing Journalism*, p. 108 (1993).

50   Procunier v. Martinez: *Procunier v. Martinez*, 416 U.S. 396 (1974).

51   *Justice Holmes's* Abrams *opinion: Abrams v. United States*, 250 U.S. 616 (1919), and discussion in Chapter 2.

55   *questions about whether responsible federal prison officials had acted unconstitutionally: Martin v. Rison*, 962 F.2d 959 (9th Cir. 1992).

56   *The* Washington Post *had challenged the no-interview rule: Saxbe v. Washington Post*, 417 U.S. 843 (1974).

4. Raymond Procunier and Robert H. Schnacke

59   Procunier v. Martinez: *Procunier v. Martinez*, 416 U.S. 396 (1974), discussed in Chapter 3.

59   *a sedition case in the McCarthy era:* Taylor, "Tried for Sedition During 'Red Scare,'" *San Francisco Chronicle*, p. B6, December 21, 2008.

62 *a federal court had found conditions there constitutionally intolerable: Ruiz v. Estelle,* 679 F.2d 1115 (5th Cir. 1982).

71 New York Times *columnist:* Anthony Lewis, "'Their Brutal Mirth,'" *New York Times,* May 20, 1991.

71 *Freedom of Information Act:* 5 U.S.C. section 552 *et seq.*

72 *I lost a case for KQED: Houchins v. KQED,* 438 U.S. 1 (1978), discussed in Chapter 6.

72 *In 1980, the Court decided the first in a series: Richmond Newspapers, Inc. v. Commonwealth of Virginia,* 448 U.S. 555 (1980).

72 *Two of the cases . . . involved death penalty prosecutions: Press-Enterprise v. Superior Court,* 464 U.S. 510 (1984); *Press-Enterprise v. Superior Court,* 478 U.S. 1 (1986).

74 *In the first execution . . . a San Francisco newspaper reported:* "Execution of Henry F. W. Mowes," *Daily Evening Bulletin,* p. 2, December 10, 1858.

75 *San Quentin execution of Lee Sing:* "'Good-bye All White Men': Lee Sing Steps Upon the Fatal Trap," *San Francisco Examiner,* p. 4, February 3, 1894.

75 *The* San Francisco Examiner *reported:* A. D. Hyman, "2 Killers Gassed; Chorus of Protest Arises at Ordeal," *San Francisco Examiner,* p. 1, December 3, 1938.

76 *Mary Crawford of the* San Francisco News-Call Bulletin: "Exclusive! Woman Sees Execution—'Barbaric,' Writer Says," *San Francisco News-Call Bulletin,* p. 1, May 2, 1960.

78 *He put his feet up, leaned back in his chair, and delivered his judgment: KQED v. Vasquez,* 18 Media L. Rptr. 2323 (N.D. Cal. 1991).

80 *KQED's CEO said:* KQED press release, "KQED will not appeal decision in First Amendment lawsuit," September 4, 1991, on file with author.

5. Earl Caldwell

83 *On June 15, 1969:* Earl Caldwell, "Black Panthers Serving Youngsters a Diet of Food and Politics," *New York Times,* June 15, 1969.

84   *One story, for example:* Earl Caldwell, "Black Panthers: 'Young Revolutionaries at War,'" *New York Times*, September 6, 1968.

84   *an agent left a message at his office: Frontline* interview of Earl Caldwell conducted July 6, 2006, http://www.pbs.org/wgbh/pages/frontine/newswar/interviews.

89   Branzburg v. Hayes: *Branzburg v. Hayes*, 408 U.S. 665 (1972).

93   *Madison was speaking about the need for* education: Letter from James Madison to W. T. Barry, August 4, 1822, in *The Founders Constitution*, Vol. 1, Chapter 18, Document 35 (University of Chicago Press).

93   *In 1974 . . . Justice Stewart:* Stewart, "Or of the Press," 26 *Hastings L.J.* 631 (1975).

93   *Anthony Lewis, the* New York Times *columnist:* Lewis, "A Preferred Position for Journalism?" 7 *Hofstra L. Rev.* 595 (1979).

95   *eloquent tribute to the press in his famous report:* James Madison, Report on the Virginia Resolutions, January, 1800.

95   *Perhaps the framers singled out the press:* see concurring opinion of Chief Justice Warren Burger in *First National Bank of Boston v. Bellotti*, 435 U.S. 765 (1978).

96   *Newspaper Publishers Association got the legislature to enact a strong law:* California Evidence Code section 1070.

96   *A virtually identical provision was added by the voters:* California Constitution, Article I, section 2(b).

97   *the Free Flow of Information Act:* Senate Bill 448, approved by the Senate Judiciary Committee on December 10, 2009.

6. Richard Hongisto

100   Pell v. Procunier: *Pell v. Procunier*, 417 U.S. 817 (1974). The defendant in this case, Raymond Procunier, is the same person who progressed from villain to hero status in Chapter 4. He had not made this transition in 1974.

100   *threaten the officials' control:* This was the same rationale, or perhaps pretext, used in Dannie Martin's case discussed in Chapter 3.

101   *his own ambivalence about the role of the press:* see Stewart, "Or

of the Press," 26 *Hastings L.J.* 631 (1974), and discussion in Chapter 5.

101   *a federal judge had found conditions there "shocking and debasing":* Brenneman v. Madigan, 343 F. Supp. 128 (N.D. Cal. 1972).

104   *unanimously ruled in KQED's favor: KQED* v. Houchins, 546 F.2d 284 (9th Cir. 1976).

105   *William Rehnquist was very conservative:* Rehnquist did not write his only strong First Amendment decision until 1988, in *Hustler* v. Falwell, 485 U.S. 46 (1988), discussed in Chapter 8.

106   *his* Branzburg *opinion: Branzburg* v. Hayes, 408 U.S. 665 (1972), discussed in Chapter 5.

110   *On June 26, 1978, the Court handed down its decision: Houchins* v. KQED, 438 U.S. 1 (1978).

112   *his book* Freedom of the Press: Bernard Schwartz, *Freedom of the Press,* pp. 30–33 (1992).

113   *In 1980, the Court decided the first of four cases: Richmond Newspapers, Inc.* v. Commonwealth of Virginia, 448 U.S. 555 (1980), discussed in Chapter 4.

114   *"Democracy dies behind closed doors": Detroit Free Press* v. Ashcroft, 303 F.3d 681 (6th Cir. 2002) (opinion of Keith, J.).

118   *We sued in federal court: Coming Up, Inc.* v. City and County of San Francisco, No. C92 3714 DLJ (N.D. Cal.); various opinions in the case are reported at 857 F. Supp. 711 (N.D. Cal. 1994), and 830 F. Supp. 1302 (N.D. Cal. 1993).

119   *indisputably protected by the First Amendment:* see *Hustler Magazine* v. Falwell, 485 U.S. 46 (1988), discussed in Chapter 8.

119   *But the Supreme Court had made it clear: Lovell* v. Griffin, 303 U.S. 444 (1938), discussed in Chapter 2.

7. Clarence Brandenburg

122   *The clear-and-present-danger test: Schenck* v. United States, 249 U.S. 47 (1919), discussed in Chapter 2.

123   *The Court struck down the Ohio law: Brandenburg* v. Ohio, 395 U.S. 444 (1969)

123 Whitney v. California: *Whitney v. California,* 274 U.S. 357 (1927), discussed in Chapter 2.

123 Dennis, *the Communist case: Dennis v. United States,* 341 U.S. 494 (1951), discussed in Chapter 2.

124 *the* Pentagon Papers *case: United States v. New York Times,* 403 U.S. 713 (1971).

124 New York Times v. Sullivan: *New York Times v. Sullivan,* 376 U.S. 254 (1964).

126 *the child pornography case: Ashcroft v. Free Speech Coalition,* 535 U.S. 234 (2002), discussed in Chapter 8.

126 *in his book* Freedom for the Thought That We Hate: Anthony Lewis, *Freedom for the Thought That We Hate,* pp. 161–67 (2007).

127 *"The remedy to be applied is more speech": Whitney v. California,* 274 U.S. 357 (1927). This principle—that the remedy for dangerous speech is not suppression but more speech—was expressly invoked by the Court in *Citizens United v. Federal Election Commission,* 558 U.S. ___ (2010), discussed in the Introduction and the Afterword.

131 *Alexander Meiklejohn . . . testified before the Senate:* testimony of Alexander Meiklejohn before Senate Judiciary Subcommittee on the Constitution, 1955, published in his book *Political Freedom: The Constitutional Powers of the People,* pp. 107–24 (1965).

8. Larry Flynt

133 *he shouted at the justices:* Larry Flynt, *An Unseemly Man: My Life as Pornographer, Pundit, and Social Outcast,* p. 192 (1996).

135 *Justice Potter Stewart famously lamented: Jacobellis v. Ohio,* 378 U.S. 184, 197 (1964).

136 *the Court decided* Miller v. California: *Miller v. California,* 413 U.S. 15 (1973).

136 *Professor Kathleen Sullivan has paraphrased the first two parts:* Kathleen Sullivan, "Girls Lean Back Everywhere: The Law of Obscenity and the Assault on Genius," *New Republic* (Sept. 28, 1992), p. 35 (book review).

136   *Even Justice Antonin Scalia has called for "reexamination" of the test:* see *Pope v. Illinois,* 481 U.S. 497 (1987).

137   *The FCC has long been empowered by Congress:* see 18 U.S.C. section 1464, prohibiting "any obscene, indecent, or profane language" on the airwaves.

137   FCC v. Pacifica Foundation: *FCC v. Pacifica Foundation,* 438 U.S. 726 (1978).

138   *the decision invalidating the Communications Decency Act and opined in a later case:* see *Reno v. ACLU,* 521 U.S. 844 (1997), invalidating the CDA; *Ashcroft v. ACLU,* 542 U.S. 656 (2004), concurring opinion of Justice Stevens, 160.

140   *the Supreme Court upheld the FCC's "fleeting expletives" policy shift:* FCC v. Fox Television Stations, Inc., 556 U.S. ____ (2009).

140   *The laws prohibit pictures of minors performing sex acts:* see 18 U.S.C. sections 2252, 2256.

140   *The Supreme Court has decided that sexually explicit pictures:* New York v. Ferber, 458 U.S. 747 (1982).

141   *a consumer cannot be prosecuted:* see Stanley v. Georgia, 394 U.S. 557 (1969).

142   *Flynt's autobiography provides clues:* Larry Flynt, *An Unseemly Man: My Life as Pornographer, Pundit, and Social Outcast* (1996).

146   *The Court handed down its decision:* Hustler Magazine v. Falwell, 485 U.S. 46 (1988).

146   *his famous* Abrams *dissent:* Abrams v. United States, 250 U.S. 616 (1919), discussed in Chapter 2.

148   *principle first espoused in the Jehovah's Witnesses cases:* see cases discussed in Chapter 2.

150   *Another* Hustler *case may make it harder:* Herceg v. Hustler Magazine, Inc., 814 F.2d 1017 (5th Cir. 1987).

9. Clinton Fein and the ACLU

155   *the Communications Decency Act of 1996:* 47 U.S.C. sections 223(a) and 223(d).

156   *the way the FCC defined indecency:* see FCC v. Pacifica Foundation, 438 U.S. 726 (1978), and discussion in Chapter 8.

160   *As* Hustler v. Falwell *and the Jehovah's Witnesses cases amply demonstrate:* see *Hustler Magazine v. Falwell,* 485 U.S. 46 (1988), discussed in Chapter 8, and the Jehovah's Witnesses cases discussed in Chapter 2.

161   *the Supreme Court decided the ACLU case: Reno v. ACLU,* 521 U.S. 844 (1997).

161   *the Court in 1915 allowed cities to censor: Mutual Film Corp. v. Ohio,* 236 U.S. 230 (1915).

161   *ruling was not overruled until 1952: Jos. Burstyn, Inc. v. Wilson,* 343 U.S. 495 (1952).

161   *Court had to decide the extent to which cable television could be regulated:* see *Turner Broadcasting System v. FCC,* 512 U.S. 622 (1994), and *Denver Area Educational Telecommunications Consortium v. FCC,* 518 U.S. 727 (1996).

162   *the FCC's regulation of radio and broadcast television:* see discussion in Chapter 8.

166   *two of the three district court judges agreed with the government: ApolloMedia Corporation v. Reno,* 19 F.Supp. 2d 1081 (N.D. Cal. 1998).

167   *the shortest First Amendment decision ever made: ApolloMedia Corporation v. Reno,* 119 S.Ct. 1450 (1999).

167   *It was now the law of the land:* Congress in its wisdom has since amended the statute, rendering it meaningless. The law now provides that it is a felony to communicate anything "obscene or child pornography" with the intent to annoy another person. 47 U.S.C. section 223(a). Of course obscene material and child pornography have long been prohibited, in any medium, so the amended provision has no independent significance.

169   *On May 13, 2002, the Court vacated: Ashcroft v. ACLU,* 535 U.S. 564 (2002).

170   *On June 29, 2004, the Supreme Court upheld the lower court's grant: Ashcroft v. ACLU,* 542 U.S. 656 (2004).

172   *the government cannot prosecute people for not wearing suspenders: ACLU v. Mukasey,* 534 F.3d 181 (3d Cir. 2008).

173   *the Court denied review. COPA was dead: Mukasey v. ACLU*, No.
       08-565 (January 21, 2009).

173   *The Supreme Court had approved laws outlawing pictures of minors:*
       New York v. Ferber, 458 U.S. 747 (1982).

173   *Justice Kennedy wrote a courageous opinion: Ashcroft v. Free Speech*
       Coalition, 535 U.S. 234 (2002).

175   Brandenburg v. Ohio: *Brandenburg v. Ohio,* 395 U.S. 444 (1969),
       discussed in Chapter 7.

175   *the Supreme Court upheld a fourth law, the Children's Internet*
       Protection Act: United States v. American Library Association, 539
       U.S. 194 (2003).

176   *by a threat to withhold a benefit:* The San Francisco Public Library
       refuses to apply for federal funding for Internet access and
       therefore does not put filters on public access computers. Its
       policy is "As with other library materials, restriction of a child's
       access to the Internet is the responsibility of the parent or legal
       guardian." Policy No. 206, adopted December, 1998. A city
       ordinance (No. 206-01) provides that the public is entitled to
       uncensored access to information available on the Internet.

177   *nicely resolved by Ann Beeson of the ACLU:* Schwartz, "Internet
       Filters Are: [Good] [Bad] [Both]," *New York Times,* July 4, 2004.

178   *That court noted that the law the government had invoked: United*
       States v. ApolloMedia Corporation, No. 99-20849 (5th Cir. June 2,
       2000).

179   *Supreme Court Justice John Marshall Harlan once said: Cohen v.*
       California, 403 U.S. 15 (1971).

180   *One of the chief purposes of the First Amendment:* see *Near v.*
       Minnesota, 238 U.S. 697 (1931) (Chief Justice Hughes: the "chief
       purpose" of the free press guaranty was to prevent prior
       restraints on publication).

180   *in the* Pentagon Papers *case: United States v. New York Times,* 403
       U.S. 713 (1971).

180   *approved the concept of an injunction: Aguilar v. Avis Rent a Car*
       System, 21 Cal. 4th 121 (1999).

181   *The headline of a review . . . states plainly:* Kenneth Baker, "His
      Art Is Not Subtle. It Can Be Hard to Take. But Clinton Fein
      Is Not Afraid to Make a Statement," *San Francisco Chronicle,*
      November 2, 2004.

182   *The printer found the images offensive:* Kenneth Baker, "2 of
      Clinton Fein's Political Works Run Afoul of His Printer's
      Policies," *San Francisco Chronicle,* October 12, 2004.

Afterword

185   *Harvard Law Professor Laurence Tribe:* Tribe, "The Constitution
      in Cyberspace: Law and Liberty Beyond the Electronic
      Frontier," address at first Conference on Computers, Freedom
      & Privacy, 1991.

185   *ReclaimDemocracy.org proposed amending the Constitution:*
      ReclaimDemocracy.org, "Supreme Court Rules Corporations
      are Free to Dominate Elections—Citizens' Movement Emerges
      to Overrule the Court," January 21, 2010. http://reclaimdemoc-
      racy.org/corporate_speech/amendment_ca.

186   *in 1969 the Court upheld the Fairness Doctrine: Red Lion Broad-
      casting Co. v. FCC,* 395 U.S. 367 (1969).

186   Miami Herald v. Tornillo: *Miami Herald v. Tornillo,* 418 U.S. 241
      (1974).

188   *vociferous opposition from the Christian right:* Direct mail from
      Rev. Lou Sheldon, Traditional Values Coalition (2009), on file
      with author.

188   *The Court in* Citizens United *invoked the same idea: Citizens
      United v. FEC,* 558 U.S. ____ (2010), discussed in Introduction.

190   *In an 1886 railroad case: Santa Clara County v. Southern Pacific
      Railroad,* 118 U.S. 394 (1886).

190   *whether corporations are persons under the Equal Protection Clause:
      Smyth v. Ames,* 169 U.S. 466, 522 (1898).

190   *the Fifth Amendment privilege against self-incrimination:* see, e.g.,
      Braswell v. United States, 487 U.S. 99 (1988); *United States v. White,*
      322 U.S. 694, 698 (1944); *Hale v. Henkel,* 201 U.S. 43 (1906).

INDEX

Abrams, Floyd, 71

Abrams v. United States, 40–41

access to government facilities, information, and proceedings right of, 71, 78, 95–96, 108, 110, 111, 114 (*see also* Freedom of Information Act; "press exceptionalism")

Adams, John, 22

advocacy, 21, 124. *See also* canvassing; incitement

of criminal activity, 41, 122–24, 126, 129–32, 175

of hateful ideas, 124, 126, 127, 152, 175

of overthrow of government, 41, 122, 123, 132

Ahmadinejad, Mahmoud, 149

Alameda County jail in Santa Rita, 101–4

Allison, Charles L., 19

American Civil Liberties Union

(ACLU), 123, 156, 160, 168, 179, 180

Stromberg and, 19–20

American Communist Party, xii

American Library Association, United States v., 175

Amsterdam, Anthony, 85

animal cruelty videos, 37, 38

"annoy," intent to, 158–61, 165

annoy.com, 158–61, 167, 178, 181

Beeson, Ann, 177

Bennett, Alex, 141

Berkowitz, Isadore, 18

Berrigan brothers, 55

bin Laden, Osama, 149

Black, Hugo L., xii, 125, 126

Black Panthers, 83–86, 88–89, 97–98. *See also* Caldwell, Earl

Blackmun, Harry, 53, 105

Bono (singer), 139, 140

Booty, Kelvin, 103, 106

ACKNOWLEDGMENTS

Thanks to my students at Berkeley and at The Fromm Institute for asking all those questions, and to my clients who lived these stories firsthand. I am grateful to Ben Bagdikian for giving me the opportunity to teach at Berkeley. Molly and Andy Turner cheerfully contributed both substantive advice and technology tips familiar to their generation but not mine; Micki Turner did too, though she's their mother.

A lot of people lent a helping hand in finding materials and people, and in talking to me about what they knew, including Earl Caldwell, Kim Corsaro, Elaine Elinson, Clinton Fein, Larry Flynt, Alexandra Gormly, Dannie Martin, Robert Moore, Jan Sluizer, Peter Sussman, and the reference librarians at Berkeley Law School. Beth Brinkmann did some great historical research and lawyering in the *KQED* case discussed in Chapter 4. Mike Traynor's astute work in Clinton Fein's cases was invaluable. My former partners Donna Brorby and Elizabeth Laporte unfailingly supported my forays into First Amendment controversies, as did the firm that kindly took me in for the last years of practice, Rogers, Joseph, O'Donnell.

Anthony Lewis inspired me. I read his *Gideon's Trumpet* (1964) at the outset of my legal career. It was the first book to explain, in terms we can all understand, how the Supreme Court actually works. His *Make No Law* (1991) is the best history of First Amendment freedoms, and I used it in my class for many years. I now use his more recent *Freedom for the Thought That We Hate* (2007). Over the years he has given me a lot of helpful suggestions, and our disagreements have always been friendly.

Among other books and materials that I found useful in various ways are: Geoffrey Stone, *Perilous Times: Free Speech in Wartime* (2004); Kathleen Sullivan and Gerald Gunther, *First Amendment Law* (1999); Freund, Sutherland, Howe, and Brown, *Constitutional Law: Cases and other Problems* (1961); Columbia School of Journalism, *Essential Liberty: First Amendment Battles for a Free Press* (1992); Brief for Respondent in *United States v. Caldwell*, No. 70-57, authored by Professor Anthony G. Amsterdam; and the *Frontline* interview of Earl Caldwell at www.pbs .org/wgbh/pages/frontiline/newswar/interviews/earlcaldwell (July 6, 2006).

Thanks to Peter Richardson at PoliPointPress for seeing that this book was worth publishing and to him and Melissa Edeburn, and to Dave Peattie and Tanya Grove at BookMatters, for almost painlessly guiding it through to publication.

ABOUT THE AUTHOR

As a lawyer for 45 years, William Bennett Turner handled the trials and appeals of many notable First Amendment and civil rights cases, and argued three cases in the U.S. Supreme Court. He has taught the First Amendment to generations of U.C. Berkeley students. He graduated from the Harvard Law School in 1963.

Other Books from PoliPointPress

The Blue Pages:
A Directory of Companies Rated by Their Politics and Practices, **2nd**
edition
Helps consumers match their buying decisions with their political values by
listing the political contributions and business practices of over 1,000 companies. $12.95, PAPERBACK.

Sasha Abramsky, Breadline USA:
The Hidden Scandal of American Hunger and How to Fix It
Treats the increasing food insecurity crisis in America not only as a matter of
failed policies, but also as an issue of real human suffering. $23.95, CLOTH.

Rose Aguilar, Red Highways: A Liberal's Journey into the Heartland
Challenges red state stereotypes to reveal new strategies for progressives. $15.95,
PAPERBACK.

John Amato and David Neiwert, *Over the Cliff:*
How Obama's Election Drove the American Right Insane
A witty look at—and an explanation of—the far-right craziness that overtook
the conservative movement after Obama became president. $16.95, PAPERBACK.

Dean Baker, *False Profits: Recovering from the Bubble Economy*
Recounts the causes of the economic meltdown and offers a progressive program for rebuilding the economy and reforming the financial system and stimulus programs. $15.95, PAPERBACK.

Dean Baker, *Plunder and Blunder:*
The Rise and Fall of the Bubble Economy
Chronicles the growth and collapse of the stock and housing bubbles and explains how policy blunders and greed led to the catastrophic—but completely
predictable—market meltdowns. $15.95, PAPERBACK.

Jeff Cohen, *Cable News Confidential:*
My Misadventures in Corporate Media
Offers a fast-paced romp through the three major cable news channels—Fox
CNN, and MSNBC—and delivers a serious message about their failure to
cover the most urgent issues of the day. $14.95, PAPERBACK.

Marjorie Cohn, *Cowboy Republic:*
Six Ways the Bush Gang Has Defied the Law
Shows how the executive branch under President Bush has systematically de-
fied the law instead of enforcing it. $14.95, PAPERBACK.

Marjorie Cohn and Kathleen Gilberd, *Rules of Disengagement:*
The Politics and Honor of Military Dissent

Examines what U.S. military men and women have done—and what their families and others can do—to resist illegal wars, as well as military racism, sexual harassment, and denial of proper medical care. $14.95, PAPERBACK.

Joe Conason, *The Raw Deal: How the Bush Republicans Plan to Destroy Social Security and the Legacy of the New Deal*

Reveals the well-financed and determined effort to undo the Social Security Act and other New Deal programs. $11.00, PAPERBACK.

Kevin Danaher, Shannon Biggs, and Jason Mark, *Building the Green Economy: Success Stories from the Grassroots*

Shows how community groups, families, and individual citizens have protected their food and water, cleaned up their neighborhoods, and strengthened their local economies. $16.00, PAPERBACK.

Kevin Danaher and Alisa Gravitz, *The Green Festival Reader:*
Fresh Ideas from Agents of Change

Collects the best ideas and commentary from some of the most forward green thinkers of our time. $15.95, PAPERBACK.

Reese Erlich, *Conversations with Terrorists:*
Middle East Leaders on Politics, Violence, and Empire

Offers critical portraits of six Middle Eastern leaders, usually vilified as terrorists, to probe the U.S. war on terror and its media reception. $14.95, PAPERBACK.

Reese Erlich, *Dateline Havana:*
The Real Story of U.S. Policy and the Future of Cuba

Explores Cuba's strained relationship with the United States, the island nation's evolving culture and politics, and prospects for U.S. Cuba policy with the departure of Fidel Castro. $22.95, HARDCOVER.

Reese Erlich, *The Iran Agenda:*
The Real Story of U.S. Policy and the Middle East Crisis

Explores the turbulent recent history between the two countries and how it has led to a showdown over nuclear technology. $14.95, PAPERBACK.

Todd Farley, *Making the Grades:*
My Misadventures in the Standardized Testing Industry

Exposes the folly of many large-scale educational assessments through an alternately edifying and hilarious first-hand account of life in the testing business. $16.95, PAPERBACK.

John Geluardi, *Cannabiz:*
The Explosive Rise of the Medical Marijuana Industry

Reveals how a counterculture movement created a lucrative medical marijuana industry with a political wing devoted to full legalization. $15.95, PAPERBACK.

Steven Hill, *10 Steps to Repair American Democracy*

Identifies the key problems with American democracy, especially election practices, and proposes ten specific reforms to reinvigorate it. $11.00, PAPERBACK.

Jim Hunt, *They Said What?*
Astonishing Quotes on American Power, Democracy, and Dissent

Covering everything from squashing domestic dissent to stymieing equal representation, these quotes remind progressives exactly what they're up against. $12.95, PAPERBACK.

Michael Huttner and Jason Salzman, *50 Ways You Can Help Obama Change America*

Describes actions citizens can take to clean up the mess from the last administration, enact Obama's core campaign promises, and move the country forward. $12.95, PAPERBACK.

Helene Jorgensen, *Sick and Tired:*
How America's Health Care System Fails Its Patients

Recounts the author's struggle to receive proper treatment for Lyme disease and examines the inefficiencies and irrationalities that she discovered in America's health care system during that five-year odyssey. $16.95, PAPERBACK.

Markos Kounalakis and Peter Laufer, *Hope Is a Tattered Flag:*
Voices of Reason and Change for the Post-Bush Era

Gathers together the most listened-to politicos and pundits, activists and thinkers, to answer the question: what happens after Bush leaves office? $29.95, HARDCOVER; $16.95 PAPERBACK.

Yvonne Latty, *In Conflict:*
Iraq War Veterans Speak Out on Duty, Loss, and the Fight to Stay Alive

Features the unheard voices, extraordinary experiences, and personal photographs of a broad mix of Iraq War veterans, including Congressman Patrick Murphy, Tammy Duckworth, Kelly Daugherty, and Camilo Mejia. $24.00, HARDCOVER.

Phillip Longman, *Best Care Anywhere:*
***Why VA Health Care Is Better Than Yours,* 2nd edition**
Shows how the turnaround at the long-maligned VA hospitals provides a blue-print for salvaging America's expensive but troubled health care system. $15.95, PAPERBACK.

Phillip Longman and Ray Boshara, *The Next Progressive Era*
Provides a blueprint for a re-empowered progressive movement and describes its implications for families, work, health, food, and savings. $22.95, HARDCOVER.

Marcia and Thomas Mitchell, *The Spy Who Tried to Stop a War:*
Katharine Gun and the Secret Plot to Sanction the Iraq Invasion
Describes a covert operation to secure UN authorization for the Iraq war and the furor that erupted when a young British spy leaked it. $23.95, HARDCOVER.

Markos Moulitsas, *American Taliban:*
How War, Sex, Sin, and Power Bind Jihadists and the Radical Right
Highlights how American conservatives are indistinguishable from Islamic radicals except in the name of their god. $15.95, PAPERBACK.

Susan Mulcahy, ed., *Why I'm a Democrat*
Explores the values and passions that make a diverse group of Americans proud to be Democrats. $14.95, PAPERBACK.

David Neiwert, *The Eliminationists:*
How Hate Talk Radicalized the American Right
Argues that the conservative movement's alliances with far-right extremists have not only pushed the movement's agenda to the right, but also have be-come a malignant influence increasingly reflected in political discourse. $16.95, PAPERBACK.

Christine Pelosi, *Campaign Boot Camp: Basic Training for Future Leaders*
Offers a seven-step guide for successful campaigns and causes at all levels of government. $15.95, PAPERBACK.

William Rivers Pitt, *House of Ill Repute:*
Reflections on War, Lies, and America's Ravaged Reputation
Skewers the Bush Administration for its reckless invasions, warrantless wire-taps, lethally incompetent response to Hurricane Katrina, and other scandals and blunders. $16.00, PAPERBACK.

Sarah Posner, *God's Profits:*
Faith, Fraud, and the Republican Crusade for Values Voters
Examines corrupt televangelists' ties to the Republican Party and unprec-edented access to the Bush White House. $19.95, HARDCOVER.

Nomi Prins, *Jacked: How "Conservatives" Are Picking Your Pocket—Whether You Voted for Them or Not*

Describes how the "conservative" agenda has affected your wallet, skewed national priorities, and diminished America—but not the American spirit. $12.00, PAPERBACK.

Cliff Schecter, *The Real McCain: Why Conservatives Don't Trust Him—And Why Independents Shouldn't*

Explores the gap between the public persona of John McCain and the reality of this would-be president. $14.95, HARDCOVER.

Norman Solomon, *Made Love, Got War: Close Encounters with America's Warfare State*

Traces five decades of American militarism and the media's all-too-frequent failure to challenge it. $24.95, HARDCOVER.

John Sperling et al., *The Great Divide: Retro vs. Metro America*

Explains how and why our nation is so bitterly divided into what the authors call Retro and Metro America. $19.95, PAPERBACK.

Mark Sumner, *The Evolution of Everything: How Selection Shapes Culture, Commerce, and Nature*

Shows how Darwin's theory of evolution has been misapplied—and why a more nuanced reading of that work helps us understand a wide range of social and economic activity as well as the natural world. $15.95, PAPERBACK.

Daniel Weintraub, *Party of One: Arnold Schwarzenegger and the Rise of the Independent Voter*

Explains how Schwarzenegger found favor with independent voters, whose support has been critical to his success, and suggests that his bipartisan approach represents the future of American politics. $19.95, HARDCOVER.

Curtis White, *The Barbaric Heart: Faith, Money, and the Crisis of Nature*

Argues that the solution to the present environmental crisis may come from an unexpected quarter: the arts, religion, and the realm of the moral imagination. $16.95, PAPERBACK.

Curtis White, *The Spirit of Disobedience: Resisting the Charms of Fake Politics, Mindless Consumption, and the Culture of Total Work*

Debunks the notion that liberalism has no need for spirituality and describes a "middle way" through our red state/blue state political impasse. Includes three powerful interviews with John DeGraaf, James Howard Kunstler, and Michael Ableman. $24.00, HARDCOVER.

For more information, please visit www.p3books.com.

About This Book

This book is printed on Cascade Enviro100 Print paper. It contains 100 percent post-consumer fiber and is certified EcoLogo, Processed Chlorine Free, and FSC Recycled. For each ton used instead of virgin paper, we:

- Save the equivalent of 17 trees
- Reduce air emissions by 2,098 pounds
- Reduce solid waste by 1,081 pounds
- Reduce the water used by 10,196 gallons
- Reduce suspended particles in the water by 6.9 pounds.

This paper is manufactured using biogas energy, reducing natural gas consumption by 2,748 cubic feet per ton of paper produced.

The book's printer, Malloy Incorporated, works with paper mills that are environmentally responsible, that do not source fiber from endangered forests, and that are third-party certified. Malloy prints with soy and vegetable based inks, and over 98 percent of the solid material they discard is recycled. Their water emissions are entirely safe for disposal into their municipal sanitary sewer system, and they work with the Michigan Department of Environmental Quality to ensure that their air emissions meet all environmental standards.

The Michigan Department of Environmental Quality has recognized Malloy as a Great Printer for their compliance with environmental regulations, written environmental policy, pollution prevention efforts, and pledge to share best practices with other printers. Their county Department of Planning and Environment has designated them a Waste Knot Partner for their waste prevention and recycling programs.

$15.95

RECEIVED

APR 0 9 2018

BY: ....